Our Haunted Travels
Volume 1
St. Augustine

Shawn and Marianne Donley

DEDICATION

This book is dedicated to all the friends and family we have met within the paranormal realm. Keep on doing what you do, and happy hunting!

CONTENTS

ACKNOWLEDGEMENTS

We would like to thank all of the National Park Historians and private tour guides in the St. Augustine area, with special consideration to those who headed the ghost tours. Without your excellent knowledge of the locations and expertise in storytelling, we may have not got involved in the paranormal at all.   People such as yourselves, the keepers of history and knowledge, are such a great asset to our society, please never stop doing what you do.
We would also like to thank Eric Altman and Marie Samuels for making us a part of Beyond the Edge Radio and encouraging us with the "Haunted Spotlight". This was the beginning of the research documentation that has now turned into "Our Haunted Travels," and without preparing for that show, we probably would have not been motivated to begin organizing and compiling all of this information into this format.

1 ABOUT THESE BOOKS

We have created this series of books for many reasons, mostly to help document our travels and adventures for ourselves. However, if we help others who share in our interests and activities, then these books hopefully will guide you as you travel and have adventures of your own.

Each chapter is dedicated to a location that we have personally visited. The chapters begin with the PANICd number for the location and address. We list some history for the location, some stories about the location, the paranormal claims about the location, and why we believe the location could be haunted. We conclude the chapter with our personal opinions and views. The photographs that you will see throughout these series of books were taken by us (mostly Marianne) and we use them to help demonstrate some of our points and document some of the things we have witnessed.

With the PANICd number, you can connect to our online database, PANICd.com, and pull up the location to find out more information with links to the various items on the Internet. You can also leave comments on the location if you have any experiences or stories to share. We may also have links to more photos that Marianne may have taken at the location as well. Sometimes she has been known to take hundreds of photos at the locations. I call her our forensic photographer.

We also include some advice as to how you can get started or even gain access to some of these locations for your own research and/or tours.

We hope you find these books educational and entertaining. We welcome any input or stories you may have to share from your travels and adventures. As always, you can get a hold of us through the PANICd.com website and let us know about your information.

In November of 2017, we started a new series on our YouTube channel called "Our Haunted Travels" which coincides with this series of books. If you would like to watch any associated video, please be sure to check out our channel at http://www.youtube.com/PANICdVideos.

2 HOW IT ALL BEGAN

The year was 2010 and we arrived with great anticipation in St. Augustine, Florida for our anniversary vacation trip. We visited this lovely town during our honeymoon in 2006 and fell in love with the history, culture, warmth, and activities that a couple with our interests were able to enjoy there. Previously, we stayed on the outskirts of town and drove in, fighting with traffic and parking issues, for all of the places we wanted to visit. This time we stayed at a bed and breakfast in town and ordered a couple of small excursions with our package, such as a late-night horse drawn buggy ride and a ride on the Schooner Freedom, both of which we highly recommend. Having a room in town, a lot of the places we wanted to visit and things we wanted to do where within walking distance and we just parked our car for the duration of our stay; which was nice.

We planned on going to a few of the places we missed during our last visit and wanted to go back to some of the ones that we already visited to fill in a few details that we had forgotten. On our arrival, check-in was a little busy, but once we got settled into our room everything just clicked into place.

When we were in St. Augustine in 2006, one of the places that we visited was the St. Augustine Lighthouse. You have probably heard of this place if you are into the paranormal. The lighthouse is one of the most haunted lighthouses in the country. At the time, we were not into ghosts at all and had no idea about the paranormal. This is not to say that we had never heard of the paranormal or had any paranormal experiences prior to that time. Marianne has been visited by her great grandmother before, and I have had my dreams and visions, but we had always just chalked them up to either some kind of weird dream or eating something we shouldn't have before bedtime.

Not many changes are made to lighthouses in four years, so this time when we visited the lighthouse, Marianne found a way to experience it differently. She found on their website that they offer a night tour called "Dark of the Moon." It was a ghost hunting tour, but we could actually go to the lighthouse and the keeper's quarters at night to see the lighthouse. We thought, "Hey, we get to see the lighthouse again, just a different way."

After dinner, we drove over to the lighthouse and pulled into the parking lot. The lighthouse entrance and gift shop were closed. There was nothing on the tickets that said where to go so, we got out of the car and walked around the grounds. We eventually found out that you were supposed to meet behind the gift shop. We made our way around to the back and there was a small group of people already there waiting. As we stood there waiting for someone to come out, and hoping that we were in the right place for the tour, we started eavesdropping on some of the other people who were waiting to take the tour as well. They were saying things like, "I hope we see one," or, "Hope to see the shadow in the tower," we looked at each other like these people were just nuts.

Marianne did do a little pre-planning for the trip (she is a picture fanatic and had wanted to be able to take pictures in the dark) and had purchased a night vision camera. It is a little handheld thing that looks like a temperature gun, but does take some pretty good night vision video. As it turns out, it can also help you get down the steps of a lighthouse when the lights are off. Marianne can attest to that. She was brave enough to go up all of the steps to the top in the dark of night. I wasn't. I don't do well with stairs and not being able to see my way back down, I would have probably taken a few other guests with me as I rolled.

Finally the doors open up and the people at the lighthouse told us that they would begin the tour shortly. They had a device for an extra $3 that you could rent that would help you detect if there was a ghost nearby. Marianne asks me, "Do you want one of them?" I said, "What? $3 to rent a device to see if there is a ghost nearby? Ummm... no thank you," and I laughed. Now, let me remind you, we knew nothing about the paranormal at this time and here I am presented with the opportunity to rent a KII meter at one of the most haunted lighthouses in America. And I said, "no." Yep, I said, "no."

Well, we then take the tour, and hear one of the most interesting stories I have ever experienced in my life. We hear the tale of the lighthouse keeper and the deaths that took place on the grounds. We toured the keeper's house and got to go upstairs where the regular day tours don't go and stand in the dark and hear more tales. Then we are released to go and investigate on our own.

Investigate? "What the hell does that mean, " I asked Marianne. She responds, "I don't know, let's go out to the lighthouse." So, we leave the keeper's quarters and all of the others seem to be talking to themselves, asking weird questions, and holding what looked like recorders. We had no idea what they were doing, but we left so that we didn't make any noise and interrupt them.

We go outside and walk around the lighthouse. Marianne decided to climb it. I told her I would hang down below and await her return. When she came back, we left for the evening and went back to our room. Again, I wish we knew then what we know now, because we probably would of stayed there until they kicked us out.

The next morning we got up and had our breakfast out in the gazebo of the B&B. We talked a little bit about the lighthouse and decided to head into town to check out some of the other locations we didn't visit before, such as Flagler College and the Oldest House. After a long, hot day of walking around, we headed back to the B&B for a little rest and to get cleaned up a little bit before we headed out for dinner.

We took a stroll down Marine Street (where our B&B was located) towards the Bridge of Lions in search of a restaurant that we simply loved when we were there before called Harry's Seafood Bar and Grill. This place hosts a courtyard where you can sit outside and listen to a small band while enjoying your meal in a very relaxing, soothing environment. Sometimes when you travel, you spin-the-wheel when it comes to finding a good place to eat and when we find a place that we like, we have a tendency to go back over and over again. Harry's was one of those places.

I grade restaurants in three categories. First, is the food good? That is super important. Second, do I have to wait to have my glass of water or ice tea to be refilled? Another important thing. In fact, at Harry's I asked for them to leave the pitcher of water and they had no issues with that. For those of you who have met me or seen my picture, I am a large man and in the Florida heat, I was a little parched. Third, do we have to wait for the bill? When I am done eating, I am ready to go on to the next adventure or to go back to my room and take a nap. I don't want to waste time sitting around waiting for my bill. Now, I joke about this rating system and I often tell Marianne that it will affect the tip of the waiter or waitress. I subtract from 20% as I wait. Alas, this is just a joke, but Harry's has never failed the rating system.

For those of you reading this in anticipation of how we got into the paranormal, please, keep reading. I am getting to the point, but you need to know the entire backstory of how things came to pass in order to appreciate how close we came to not getting into the paranormal.

After dinner, we decided that we would take our horse and buggy ride around town. We have been there before and were looking for different ways to see the sights. The buggy ride was a way to just sit back and hear some of the local history from someone who lives in the city, as well as, take a little break from the walking. We climbed aboard and started off. I wish I could tell you the name of the driver or even the name of the horse; however, I am writing this six years after it happened and some of those little details have a tendency to slip your mind. Even "The Vault", Marianne's mind, does not remember the names either. As we rode through town, the driver sat sideways in her seat. She would watch where the horse was going, but would also look back at us and give us some history of the different locations we passed.

At the time, we had no belief or interest in the paranormal, even after the ghost tour at the lighthouse the night before. Yet, as we went along, the driver would say, "Yep, and this place is haunted, yep and that place is haunted…" We would just look at each other and kind of roll our eyes. I recall, faintly, rounding one bend and seeing a group of people walking. They were following this guy dressed in period clothing and carrying a lantern. The driver looked back and asked us, "Have you been on a ghost walk yet?" We both kind of snickered and replied, "Oh, no, that is not for us." She said, "Oh, well you should think about it. If nothing else, those guys have great history and stories about the different places they stop…" Again, we just kind of blew it off.

After the buggy ride was over, we said our goodbyes, provided a tip to the courteous driver, and started our journey back to our room. It was late at this point and the little town was starting to close up for the evening. In the distance, we saw a few groups of people walking around following someone carrying a lantern. Marianne asked me, "What do you think about doing one of those tours, you know, for something different?" I gave her my typical, I'm tired let's talk about it later response, "I don't know honey, we'll see."

The following morning we got up again and had breakfast in the gazebo. That day, our ride on the Schooner Freedom was planned. Due to the heat, they moved the scheduled ride to later in the afternoon. This left our morning and early afternoon somewhat open, so we took advantage of the time and visited the Spanish Military Hospital (which was closed), The Old St. John's

Jail, and Henry Flagler's grave site. We also stopped at the Castillo De San Marcos Fort and they were putting on a musket demonstration, which was pretty exciting. We also witnessed them firing the cannons, shooting bread out into the bay.

Not to discount the ride on the schooner, because it was awesome and a very memorable event, but I will skip ahead to the following day. During breakfast, Marianne asked me again what I thought about taking one of those ghost walks that night. Being more rested and refreshed, I agreed. "Why not?" was my reply. Marianne called and scheduled us to be on one of tours. We spent the day visiting a couple of other places and finally was able to get into the Spanish Military Hospital which Marianne was looking forward to visiting. They have period medical instruments on display which is something that really excites her scientific and somewhat creepy mind. After we were in the building for a few minutes, something happened. We now believe that Marianne may have had a paranormal experience, which I will explain in more detail in the Spanish Military Hospital Chapter. However, it was what happened that night that may have changed our lives and opened our eyes.

That night we took our very first "official" ghost walk. The ghost tour at the lighthouse we had taken a couple of days previous was extremely informative about the history of the lighthouse and what happened there. They really did not go into paranormal investigating or ghost hunting though. That was not the case with ghost walk. Before we began the walk, the tour guide explained how to take as many pictures as possible, what to look for while we were in the different locations, how to open your senses for certain feelings, and what we might experience. Again, we were not into the paranormal, but hey, let's just play along and do what they are saying just to see if we experience anything.

The first stop on the tour was the Spanish Military Hospital again. Although we toured the location earlier, it was quite interesting to visit the location at night, with the lights out. As we stood there in the dark, I found a location where I could stand in front of the blowing air conditioning to try and cool off. I recall it being extremely hot and humid outside. The cool air was such a relief. As the tour guide went on with his story, I recorded the whole thing on the night vision camera that we had. I wasn't really paying much attention to the screen of the camera, in fact I wasn't really even paying much attention to the tour guide. The cold air coming from the unit pretty much had my full attention.

I don't remember all of the stops that we made during this walk, and I don't remember the order of them either. I do remember stopping at the Castillo de San Marcos again, the city gates, and the city graveyard. We also went into the old drug store. The main thing I remembered about the walk were the stories being very captivating.

Every time the tour guide would finish with the history, he would discuss the tragedy that happened at the location. Whether it was a murder, suicide, or something else dark, the story always ended with information on hauntings and sightings of previous guests or tour guides at that location. No matter what the guide was saying, I remember hanging on his every word in anticipation as to what he was going to say next.

At the end of the tour, it was extremely late. We had a ways to go to walk back to our room, yet we just couldn't get enough of the tour. The tour guide was standing around looking at photographs that others had taken on their digital cameras. He had asked to see if anyone captured anything during the evening. We were standing there looking through our photos and I started looking through the night vision camera at the videos that I recorded. Something showed up at the Spanish Military Hospital. The camera has a very small screen, but I showed it to the tour guide anyways. He said that what I captured was actually one of the claims that they had at the location, but I should look at it more closely on the computer for sure.

After everyone had left, I made the move that actually sparked off our journey into paranormal investigations. I went back to the tour guide and asked him, "What is one of the most haunted locations that you are aware of in the city?" He response was, "Definitely the Tolomato Cemetery, which is next to the old drug store." The funny thing was, the cemetery was not on the walk. It was mentioned during the walk while we were in the drug store, but they do not include the cemetery as part of the walk. He went on to say, "I don't even go by there at night."

Well of course, we now had to walk past the cemetery on our journey back to our room. Little did we know, what we would capture at this cemetery would change our lives and set us on one great big adventure.

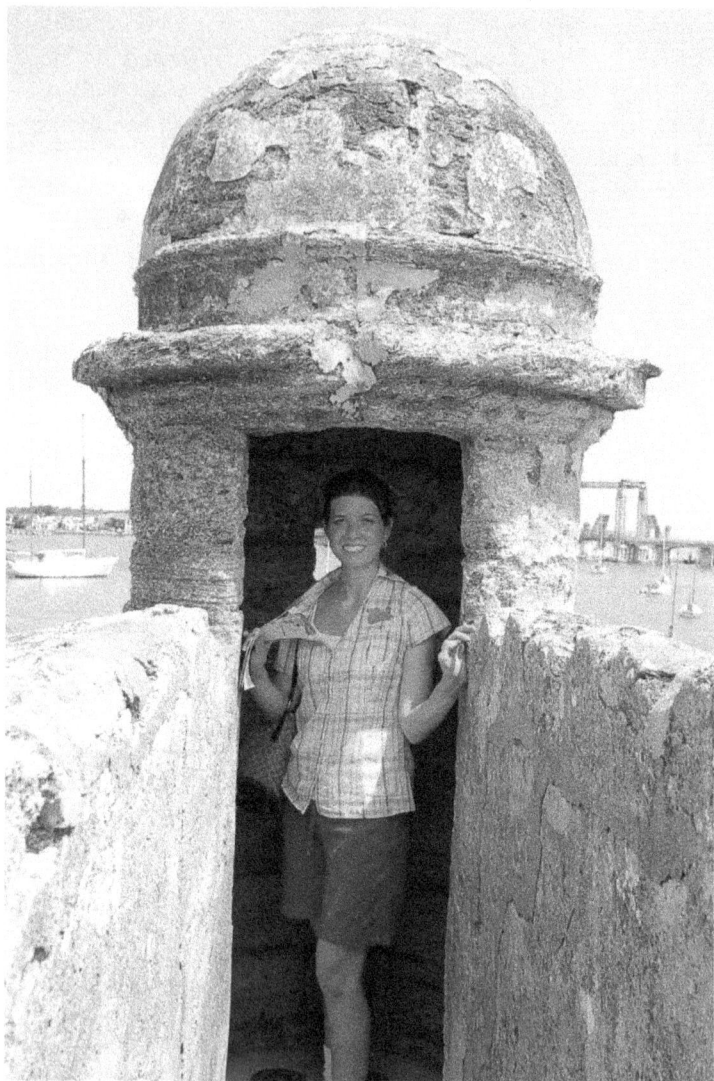

3 ST. AUGUSTINE LIGHTHOUSE

PANICd#: 1060

81 Lighthouse Avenue
St. Augustine, FL 32080

A Little History

The St. Augustine Lighthouse is not the first light station at this location. According to the location's website, in the late 1500's there was a Spanish watchtower built where the current lighthouse sits. The watch tower was made of wood and had a flame at the top, which dates the structure as being one of the first lighthouses on the location. In 1824, there was a lighted tower that was built from the locally mined rock, coquina. By 1870, the light tower was threatened by shoreline erosion. The United States Congress commissioned to build the current structure for $100,000. The current tower was built in 1874 and the Old Spanish Watchtower was destroyed by a storm in 1880.

The current lighthouse tower is constructed of Alabama brick and Philadelphia iron. It is the oldest surviving brick structure in St. Augustine. A brick keeper's quarters was added in 1876. Lighthouse keepers and assistants lived in the quarters until the light was automated in 1955.

The St. Augustine Lighthouse reaches 165 feet above sea level and required 219 steps. At the top, a first order Fresnel lens serves as the beacon. The St. Augustine lens boasts 370 hand-cut glass prisms which are arranged in a beehive shape is twelve feet tall, six feet in diameter and weighing in at 2 tons.

In 1980, the Junior Service League of St. Augustine,

Inc. began a campaign to restore the keeper's house that was destroyed by a vandal's fire in 1970. The house was opened to the public as a museum in 1988. The Junior Service League with the assistance of the U.S. Coast Guard went on to restore the tower as well and they performed the first ever Fresnel lens repair in the world to save the lens that was damaged by a vandal's bullet. In 1993, the tower was also opened to visitors on a daily basis.

In 2000, a visitor center was built and in July 2002 the U.S. Coast Guard transferred the deed for the tower to the St. Augustine Lighthouse and Museum, Inc. This was done in accordance with the pilot program of the National Historic Lighthouse Preservation Act of 2000. In addition, the Coast Guard turned over the first-order Fresnel lens to the museum.

Between 2014 and 2016, the museum purchased the additional 6.5 acre light station property. In 2016, they began construction of a 2500 sq. ft. Maritime Archaeology and Education Center and began restorations of the WWII barracks and Jeep maintenance garage.

Ghostly Encounters, Stories, and/or Folklore

There has always been something that draws me to lighthouses. Maybe it is the solitary lifestyle of the lighthouse keeper or even just the responsibilities they are charged with in order to keep the waters around the area safe for oncoming vessels, but I have always been drawn to lighthouses and researching their history.

There are a number of paranormal encounters to be had at the lighthouse property. Several individuals have met their demise here. There have been seven people who are known to have died on the lighthouse grounds: three light keepers, a keeper's wife, and three young girls. A few of these deaths are reported to be of natural causes, however, one was reportedly a keeper who fell to his death from the original lighthouse in 1859 and two of the girls died in a tragic drowning accident. The paranormal activity at the location suggests that these individuals and a few others may never have left.

One spirit that may be encountered is of one of the keepers who is generally encountered near the top of the tower. Even though he's been dead for more than a century, people believe that this is the presence of Joseph Andreu. His presence at the lighthouse could be explained by the fact that he fell to his death while painting the outside of the tower. His spirit seem never to have left and is often seen looking out from the top. Others think that his shadow is the one that is seen inside the tower looking down at those climbing up. Could this be some kind of warning?

Another of the very well-known ghosts of the Lighthouse are those of the two young sisters, and daughters of the tower construction supervisor, who died on the property. Hezekiah Pity was hired to renovate the tower in the late 1800s. His daughters, Eliza and Mary, were playing inside a cart that was being used to carry materials back and forth to the lighthouse. The cart unfortunately broke free, and the cart slid, along with the girls still inside, into the bay, sending the poor girls to their untimely and watery death.

Most days since the accident, the girls can be heard laughing at the top of the tower late at night. Others have spotted a girl, thought to be Eliza moving about the light station grounds. It is believed to be Eliza as the girl is wearing a blue dress; like the one Eliza reportedly was wearing when she died. The girls have also been seen playing together around the grounds late into the night.

Staff members have reported additional paranormal activity around the property as well. Over the years, the smell of a cigar has been detected by many, including staff members and guests throughout the grounds, especially in the keeper's quarters and basement. One of the lighthouse's first keepers was a man named Peter Rasmussen. He was known for his love of cigars and for being very meticulous about keeping the grounds well taken care of. They also often hear footsteps like someone climbing the tower, when no one else is in the tower. Could this be the cigar of Peter as he is gathering his supplies and tools to work on the lighthouse? Could the footsteps be his as he moves about the property taking care of odds and ends?

Some additional reports made by staff are that before leaving for the night they will lock the door at the top of the tower, but when they return in the morning to open up, the door is already opened while the door at the bottom of the lighthouse was still locked. The lighthouse staff also reports that chairs have been moved or overturned in the keeper's house and that various items in the gift shop get moved or go missing, only to reappear later. Music boxes have also been known to turn on by themselves. Is this perhaps Eliza and Mary or one of the other lighthouse keepers' children?

In the light keeper's quarters people often report that they feel cold or that the figure of a tall man has appeared before them, and then disappeared. We have also heard reports of mysterious wet footprints that appear on the cement in the basement of the keeper's quarters only to disappear a few moments later. Could these be the footprints of the little girls who drowned or the man that has been reported to be hanging around the water cisterns in the basement? And who is the tall man? One of the keepers or a construction worker?

Paranormal Claims

- Shadows and a hazy male figure have been seen in the tower and climbing the steps.
- Things have been moved around in the gift shop as if someone was playing with them.
- Strange sounds and noises heard coming from the tower when nobody was in it.
- There is often the smell of cigars within the keeper's house.
- Sounds of someone shuffling in the gravel outside the lighthouse can be heard.
- An apparition of a woman has been seen walking the grounds and on the lighthouse stairway.
- The sounds of two young girls playing can be heard in the tower late at night.

- The apparition of a young girl has been seen wearing a blue velvet dress and blue hair bow that she may have been wearing when she died.
- The figures of two little girls can sometimes be seen standing on the lighthouse catwalk.
- There is a large, dark male spirit that hangs around the water collecting cisterns in the basement of the keeper's house.
- The apparition of the original lighthouse keeper has been seen late at night walking around the property.
- Cold spots and a presence can be felt in the basement of the keeper's house.
- Chairs have been moved in the keeper's quarters.
- Wet footprints appear and then disappear from a corner in the basement of the keeper's quarters.

Potential of Haunting

What could be causing the continued activity at this location? Well, if you analyze the history and stories that are told surrounding the property, one does not have to wonder very much.

The little girls who suddenly and traumatically died on the property could be coming back because they are not aware that they have died. We never want to think that children do not automatically pass on, but there are several theories that state that those who are not aware that they have passed can be locked in limbo at the location where they died. There have not been any other reports of these little girls other than on the property of the lighthouse and grounds. This theory can also be the same for the man who fell from the top of the tower. Does he realize that he died from his fall?

Another theory that can be used here can be associated with the is the man who is reported to be the meticulous groundskeeper. Some paranormal investigators and researchers believe in a theory of "free will." This theory means that once you pass on, you have the ability to come back and visit a location that you enjoyed on earth. It is reported that he took care of the property for many years, so it would make sense that if he did want to come back, why not come back to a location that he enjoyed?

St. Augustine's geographical location is something else you have to consider. St. Augustine and the property the lighthouse sits on is surrounded by moving water and built on top of coquina stone. Coquina is limestone which is known to keep and trap paranormal activity. Moving water is thought to generate energy that entities can pull from in order to manifest. Could the water that is surrounding the lighthouse be one big huge spirit generator? We believe that this is the case for the entire area of St. Augustine.

Our Experiences and Opinions

As I mentioned in the chapter "How it All Began," this was our very first ghost tour. At the time, we had no idea what we were doing or even what was going on. We passed up on the opportunity to rent a KII meter at one of the most haunted lighthouses in the country. I have not been back to this location yet since my full-fledged dedication to investigating and researching paranormal activity began, but you can bet that when I return, I will be stocked and packed for ghosts.

Climbing and descending the lighthouse is not for the faint of heart. Marianne had a challenge coming back down in the dark, even using the night vision camera to help. Be warned that climbing the stairs and coming back down a lighthouse is a challenge even with the lights on. If you climb up in the dark, make sure you have a flashlight or something to come back down.

After being on several ghost tours throughout the country, we have to say that the tour at this lighthouse is among the best run that we have attended. Not only did they spend time going over the stories and hot spots at the location, they also gave you time to go off by yourself to perform your own investigating.

We wish we could report some more findings of ours for this location, but alas, we were novices and really didn't even know what to look for let alone find it. Maybe we will be able to do so next time…when we return.

4 SPANISH MILITARY HOSPITAL

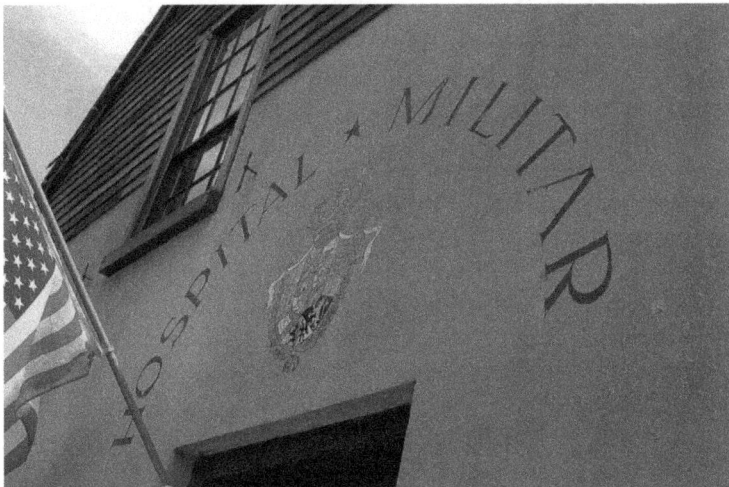

PANICd#: 1001

3 Aviles
St. Augustine, FL 32084

A Little History

This Spanish Military Hospital Museum is a replica of what was standing at this location during the Second Spanish Colonial Period in St. Augustine. Although it is reconstructed, there are many original, period dated artifacts within the building and the land on which it sits is the exact location of the original building complex on Aviles Street (aka Hospital Street). The building is a reconstruction as the original burned down, though the original foundation was discovered during an archaeological excavations. The west wing of the building (built by the Spanish) burned down in 1818. The East wing (built by the British) burned down in 1895. Both wings were reconstructed, but today only the west wing reconstruction (built from archived Spanish records) remains as the east wing reconstruction was torn down in 1960.

The museum has several rooms that would of been at the early hospital from the surgeon's office (apothecary) to the ward room. When you walk inside this building it is as if you step back in time to witness what medical practices were like during the 18th century. There is even a Mourning Room, where patients were moved prior to passing on to the other side. It is in this room were a priest would come into the hospital and bless the dying. Could you imagine waking up and noticing that they are moving you over to this room?

Inside the museum you can view many different tools and medicines that were used during the late 1700s and early 1800s, some that look like torture devices. These were the tools though that were used to help deliver medical treatments to the various patients for many years. Also available is a look into how the apothecary would make ancient remedies and medicines. The apothecary would of been the only person permitted to prescribe medicines to the patients and on the grounds both then and now is a garden to grow various plants used for medicinal purposes called a herbarium. The plants harvested from this garden are plants that would have been grown in the days of original hospital and would of been used as the ingredients for the medicines along with some crushed insects etc.

On the day tour, you will witness guides dressed in period clothing and they will gladly explain what life was like in the hospital. After the tour, you will have a better appreciation for being alive in today's society as some of the practices of medicine taking place within the hospital which could be considered quite medieval in nature today.

This photo was taken just prior to Marianne having her

"experience" during the day tour.

Ghostly Encounters, Stories, and/or Folklore

Over time, several residents, employees, and patients began to report the feeling of something "evil" and "frightening" through the building, especially within the patient ward. The evil presence seemed to hang in the air frightening patients and running off specialists that were hired to treat the sick and the dying. Most believed that this was attributed to all of the death that had occurred in or around the location. However, when the city began to tear down the building and the street in front in order to replace the water lines, what they had found was astonishing to all. It halted the project and other plans were made for the water lines.

What they found was a burial ground in the middle of the road in front the building. At first, workers thought that this was left over from the hospital, since it was widely known that limbs and body parts from amputations would just be thrown out in the street. However, a research group determined that the burial ground belonged to the Timucuan people (a group of Native Americans that were native to the area of St. Augustine in the earliest years of history.) It is also believed that part of that burial ground was under the structure of the hospital itself.

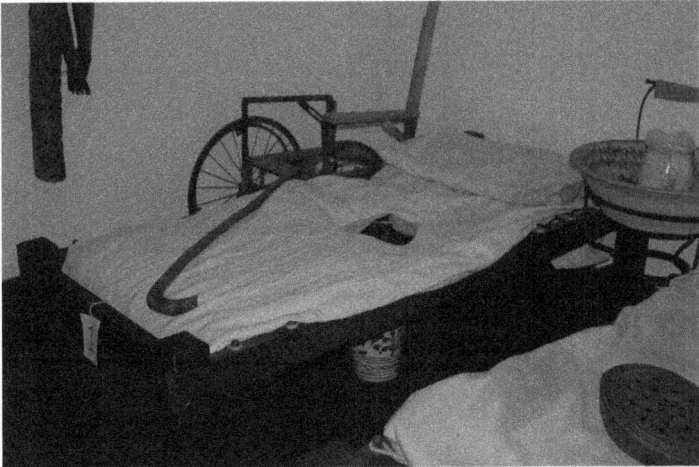

The Ward.   This is the room we were in when we captured our orb during the Ghost Tour.   (see video on PANICd.com)

Paranormal Claims

- Strange balls of light reported in the Ward room.
- Voices and whispers heard in Ward room.
- Footsteps are heard both downstairs and upstairs.
- A bucket in ward room moved across the room during an evening ghost tour.
- People have been touched, scratched, and even bitten on more than one occasion.
- Strange smells have been reported.
- Full bodied apparitions have been seen inside and also outside the building.
- Doors open and close by themselves. The front door has been unlocked by unseen hands many times.
- Objects have been thrown at people.
- People have reported getting physically ill near or

within the surgeon's room.

Potential of Haunting

There are a several reasons that would explain why this location is haunted. First is that this location was a previous military or field hospital. If you consider the emotions and the state of mind the patients were in when they were brought to this location after a battle, not knowing if they were going to survive or lose some body part(s), that energy is not positive in any way. We have reviewed many cases from field hospitals all over the country and almost all of them have some kind of paranormal claims.

Next you want to consider the loss of life that has taken place within the walls. No one from this realm truly knows how many have lost their lives here as this information has been lost to the ages. We certainly can not determine who moved on to the next realm, or which entities who have chosen to remain on earth and not move on in fear of judgment either.

Another major contributor would be the disturbed burial ground. Native American burial grounds that are disturbed are rated among the highest areas to have paranormal claims. The building, grounds, and street in front is known to be located right on top of an ancient burial ground which could explain the negative or evil haunts throughout the building.

Lastly, circling back to the idea of being a military hospital, we want to consider amputations and battle surgeries. During both the day tour and the ghost tour they talked about how many body parts were amputated and just thrown outside into the street. There is a possibility that entities could be coming back to this location looking for their missing limbs. Also, you need to consider that during the time period that the hospital was active, there was not much used in the way of anesthetic. Patients were awake and alert when body parts were removed. Those events could lead to the possibilities of residual haunts, since that would definitely expel some traumatic energy into the area.

The Mourning Room.

Our Experiences and Opinions

We believe that we both had paranormal experiences when we were at this location. The first one was had by Marianne during the day. She really wanted to take the day tour to see all of the medical gadgets from the time period, but when she entered the surgeon's room, she immediately became overwhelmed with something that made her nauseous and dizzy and she had to sit down for a little bit and drink some water. We don't know what this was since she was already in the building for a while before it happened, meaning it wasn't a change in the temperature from the heat outside and the air conditioning inside. It just came on all of a sudden and it was just too much for her to handle. She described it as, "an immediate feeling of being drained of all of her energy." After resting for a bit, outside of the surgeon's room, she was fine and able to carry on with the tour throughout the rest of the building.

Later that evening, during a ghost tour, I was standing recording the tour guide with my back to the blowing air conditioner. If you have never experienced Florida in July, let me tell you, it is hot. Even at night. To find a way to cool off, I looked for the blowing cold air as soon as we entered. During the presentation by the tour guide, who was dressed in period clothing and putting on a little show (which is a great for kids to learn history), I really wasn't paying much attention. I was just standing there, enjoying the cool breeze and recording him on our night vision camera while he was talking. Later on when we reviewed the recording, we noticed that I captured a orb pass in front of the camera. We analyzed this recording over and over, and debunked that it was not an insect since there air conditioner was blowing hard and it could of not of been dust since it came in from the left and passed out of view to the right as quickly as it came into view while the air conditioner was blowing from behind me and not one side or the other. This could of been one of the energy orbs that people claim to capture or see within the building.

These two events were probably our first paranormal experiences that we can remember now that we are investigators. Although, there could have been many more, we just didn't realize that they were happening. The more and more we research and study paranormal claims and stories, we realize that people could be experiencing paranormal activity all the time and are just not aware of what is going on around them.

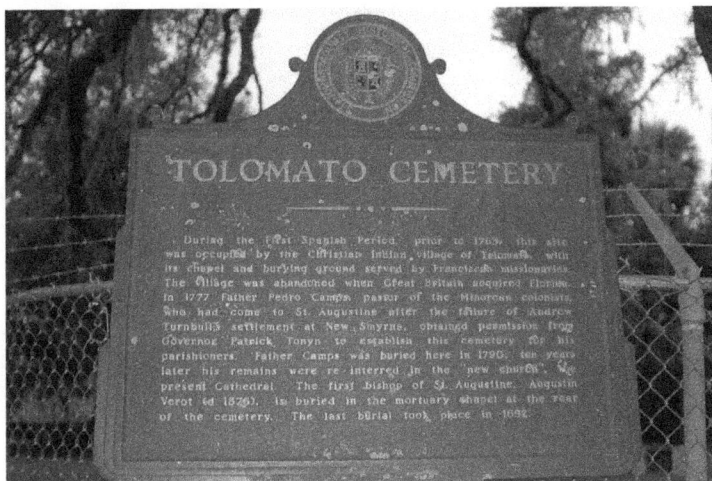

PANICd#: 1002

Cordova Street
St. Augustine, FL 32084

A Little History

The Tolomato Cemetery is the oldest cemetery in the State of Florida, dating back to the First Spanish Period (1565-1763). It has a long and illustrious history. The cemetery has changed ownership several times from the Spanish to the German Catholics, to a large group of Minorcan indentured laborers. Burials in the cemetery have stopped and started several times over the years as the ownership of the cemetery changed hands.

By 1811, the Spanish had created a formal plan for the cemetery. The Library of Congress holds a copy of a Spanish drawing of the cemetery from this period, making Tolomato the first planned cemetery in Florida.

Burials at all St. Augustine cemeteries ceased in 1884 when the city prohibited burials within the city limits for health reasons. It is known that a few secret burials took place at the cemetery in the years following this ban and the last burial at the cemetery was actually in 1892.

According to records, there are more than 1,000 souls interred within the walls of this cemetery, which is less than an acre in size, including Christian Native Americans and people from far off places including Spain, Africa, Italy, Greece, Corsica, Germany, Ireland, Haiti, Cuba and Canada, a former governor, Fr. Varela, Bishop Verot, and civil war veterans from both the North and South. Hundreds of the identified burials are those of the Minorcans, the ancestors of many St Augustine residents. Even with the large number of interments, there are actually only about 100 grave markers. The oldest marker (in the entire state of Florida) is a 16 year old girl from Philadelphia, Elizabeth Forrester, who died in 1798.

The grounds hold a small white chapel that was originally built to hold the remains of Fr. Felix Varela, originally buried here in 1853. It now sits empty as his remains were moved in 1912 to Havana to Aula Magna near Havana University, but the grave marker still remains. He is currently being considered for canonization.

The cemetery is the official property of the Cathedral-Basilica of St. Augustine and is cared for by the Tolomato Cemetery Preservation Association since its creation in August of 2010.

Ghostly Encounters, Stories, and/or Folklore

We featured this location on our radio segment The Haunted Spotlight and although this is not a paranormal related story, it is quite stunning. We found this story on a blog site when we were researching for the show. We refer to the story as The Messy Mass.

As the story goes, one of the bishops that served the faithful Catholics in St. Augustine passed away during a very hot summer. He was so popular that his funeral was delayed for several days until mourners from across the eastern United States and as far away as Cuba could come to pay their respects. In order to keep the body from deteriorating, it was sealed in a metal-lined, airtight coffin fitted with a glass window. Back then there was no air conditioning, so you can imagine the temperatures inside that coffin.

Also in those days, travel was slow. Almost two weeks had passed before the bishop's staff decided that they had given the mourners enough time to travel to the area. Hundreds of people were packed into the small chapel at the cemetery while the service took place.

During the service, a strange noise started to come from the coffin and it began to vibrate. The attendees watched in fear and amazement. Was the bishop coming back to life in front of their eyes? Suddenly there was a thunderous cracking noise and the coffin split open at its seams. The body of the bishop had swollen so much from extensive decomposition and the tremendous heat of the Florida weather that his body burst into pieces, spraying the attendants with his innards and soaking the whole chapel with the stench of rotting flesh.

Another non-paranormal story that we found is about the Apopinax Tree. This story is attributed to a man named Colonel Joseph Smith. During his first week in St. Augustine, he met a couple at a party and they became fast friends. They planned on meeting the following night, but the woman fell terribly ill and as it would happen, she was pronounced dead within the week. The husband invited the colonel to attend the funeral and asked him to walk in the funeral procession.

The family had a tradition where the deceased would be placed into a chair and carried to the cemetery. The beautiful young woman was placed in a chair and they carried her through town to what was going to be her final resting place in Tolomato Cemetery. As they carried her and passed underneath an Apopinax tree located in the cemetery, a branch punctured the skin on her forehead. This caused the body to begin to bleed. Colonel Smith, who had been observing the dead woman, believed that when she hit the tree he saw her blink.

The colonel insisted that everyone bring the woman

back down to the ground so that they could investigate the body. When they did, they noticed that she was breathing, very shallowly, but she was still alive. They then broke up the procession and rushed her back home. To everyone's amazement, she made a full recovery and lived for another 6 years. If the Colonel was not in the procession, the girl probably would of been buried alive.

Skipping ahead another 6 years, the woman died. Again, she was paraded to the Tolomato Cemetery, just as she had before. This time the husband shouted to not bring her anywhere near the Apopinax tree, stating that he couldn't handle it if the woman was still alive this time. Some people claim that she was laid out in her home for at least a week before the funeral procession began, just to make sure. This time it was truly believed that she was dead and she was buried.

The last story that we found is that of a small boy reported to be haunting the gates of the cemetery. On November 29th, 1977, a young boy named James P. Morgan was playing up in the oak tree just inside the cemetery gates and he lost his grip. He fell to the ground, hit his head, and died almost instantly. This was around the date of his 5th birthday. (This was not the legendary banker and business tycoon, but some claim that the boy was named after him.)

Young James is buried near that oak tree and it is said that some people, especially children, can see him happily running around the tree and nearby areas. There are several children who have reported to their parents that a small boy dressed in period clothing asked them to come into the cemetery and play with him.

There are many who claim that there to see a woman in white roaming around amongst the grave markers. Some say she is wearing a bridal gown, others simply indicates that when she is seen, a wave of sadness washes over them. Others do not see her, but instead insist that there is a dark presence associated with the cemetery. The tour guide who warned us about the cemetery's dark presence lives in St. Augustine. He conducts paranormal investigations and ghost tours. We were told point blank, "I will never go down there by that cemetery." These dark presences could be those of the Native Americans who are buried in this cemetery trying to get out or they could be those who weren't native to the United States trying to get back to their homelands.

Paranormal Claims

- Voices and whispers are heard coming from the cemetery.
- Misty lights and orbs have been reported around the trees.
- People have reported the feeling of being watched.
- Shadows have been reported.
- A dark shadowy figure has been reported to chase people away from the cemetery.
- The apparition of a woman in a white wedding dress has been seen walking around looking at the graves as if she was in search of something.
- The apparition of a small boy has been reportedly seen by several children asking them to come play with him.
- Men in priestly garb can sometimes be seen floating near the chapel, perhaps bemoaning the disturbance of their once eternal slumber.

Potential of Haunting

I am glad that I added this section to each chapter, since these are the discussions that I like to have with other investigators. As someone who is dedicated to the theory of lifelong learning, I find educated discussions to be very intriguing; especially when you are discussing proposed theories.

One of our theories behind the haunting at this location is related to the Native Americans buried in the cemetery who were forced to convert to the Catholic religion. We were told the story after our ghost tour when we stayed around and talked with the tour guide. He told us that there were a group of Native Americans that were forced to convert by one of the local priests. They did so since they feared for their lives and persecution. Yet, they never fully practiced as active Catholics. They just went through the paces to satisfy the priest. At the time of their deaths, they were buried within the cemetery. It is possible that these spirits are seeking a more traditional Native American internment and will remain restless, forced to roam the Earth until they have one. This could explain the angry spirits that affect people when they are in or around the cemetery.

The ghost bride that roams the cemetery could be a spirit in search a lost loved one. We have heard many stories of the same type of haunting, where a bride who was promised in marriage never experienced their time at the altar and they are cursed to roam the earth in search of their betrothed.

As for the ghost of the little boy, why is he still there lingering? The story is intriguing, especially with him asking other children to come and play with him. Does he think that he cannot leave the confines of the cemetery? Falling from a tree accidentally would cause a sudden traumatic death as well. Does he not realize that he passed away? We definitely want to go back to this location and perform an EVP (Electronic Voice Phenomenon) at the gate to see if we can communicate with him.

Our Experiences and Opinions

Although I mentioned that it all started during the ghost tour of the St. Augustine Lighthouse, the Tolomato Cemetery is the actual location where we captured our first EVP; though at the time, we had no clue that we did.

Later, as we began to get into more paranormal research, we started a website called PANICd.com. As I began to add locations to the database, a major piece was missing. We needed evidence. I remembered the video from the Spanish Military Hospital. I pulled that up on the computer and added it to the database. As I was going through the files, I came across some video that we recorded with the night vision camera at the Tolomato Cemetery. Remember that ghost tour guide said that he wouldn't walk down there at night? Well, we did. We walked past the cemetery on our way back to the bed and breakfast, stopping for a minute to record some video.

I was watching the videos on the computer with my headphones on, so as not to disturb Marianne, and sure enough, we had captured an EVP. Although the camera was just pointing at a headstone through a fence at the time, you can hear a whisper saying, "Hey, look... look over there (or here)." If you would like to hear the EVP, you can pull up Tolomato Cemetery in PANICd.com and click on the evidence tab.

Only Marianne and myself were present at the cemetery when we captured the EVP and it was about 1:00 AM. There was no one else around or out on the street at the time. After hearing that, I was hooked. Even Marianne, the skeptic, could not argue that one. We both knew we were the only ones there...living individuals at least.

Tolomato Cemetery was the location where we captured our very first EVP on camera. You can listen to this EVP on the PANICd.com website. This is one of the locations that started our adventures into paranormal research and investigations.

PANICd#: 1890

102 Orange St
St. Augustine , FL 32084

A Little History

One of the more impressive landmarks that you see as you enter the town of St. Augustine is the Old City Gate and Wall. The original wall was built in the early 1700s to help fortify the town and the townspeople from attacks.

For almost 150 years, St. Augustine was attacked and taken over by various governments. Townspeople would spend several days, sometimes months, in the Castillo de San Marcos only to come out and see that their town was devastated. Burning, looting, and various battles, would all take their toll on homes throughout the town. It was determined that a protective wall needed to be built to help protect the town.

Taking design plans from a fort, a large wall was built around the town made from local palmetto logs and coquina stone. It stretched from the fort down to the river and around the other side of the town. There were six spots built into the wall called redoubts to provide locations for placing artillery. They called this the Cubo Line.

For more than 100 years, the wall helped protect the city, although sections had to be reinforced and repaired. Major construction projects took place during the 1730s and again in 1808. The last known time the walls were used was during the Second Seminole War at which time Seminoles attacked, but were unable to get to the city itself. They did not get past the Cubo Line.

The Old City Gate itself is considered a landmark in St. Augustine. Constructed of coquina in 1808, it was built at the time of the last reconstruction of the Cubo Line and at one time it was the only entrance to the city. The gate columns still stand today and reconstructed sections of the Cubo line adjoin them to the east and west. It was restored by the National Park Service in 1965 via the mission 66 program. They are currently 24.5 ft. square towers of plastered coquina. The gate is sometimes called the La Leche Gate as it lead to the Chapel of Our Lady of La Leche.

Ghostly Encounters, Stories, and/or Folklore

Many people say the city gates are haunted due to the yellow fever epidemic that broke out in 1821. For over 100 years, St. Augustine experienced a time with no major diseases or deaths due to mass sickness. However, when Florida became a new territory for the United States, many flocked to the city to seek their fortune and fame. During that time, a little girl was found dead wearing a white dress, lying right at the entrance of the Old City Gate. Nobody came forward to claim her, but some say her name was Elizabeth. She was later buried in an unmarked mass grave in the nearby Huguenot Cemetery.

We found a possible backstory to this. During the time of the epidemic, if there was someone found in your home with yellow fever, you were driven from the town and your house was burnt down so the disease would not spread further. They claim that little Elizabeth's parents did not want to leave town, so they left her at the city gates to avoid any detection of the disease in their home.

There are those who say if you walk near the city gates in the early morning hours, you can see her dancing by the gates. This is one of the most famous ghost stories in St. Augustine.

Paranormal Claims

- Many have photographed orbs in the area around the gates.
- An apparition of a little girl dressed in white has been seen late at night.

Potential of Haunting

There is a paranormal theory that leads to the haunting of the Old City Gates is unmarked graves. Those who are not interred correctly may be cursed to roam the earth as spirits. This seems to be the case with little Elizabeth. She has been seen late at night dancing around the gates and many have taken photographs of orbs throughout the area. Could these orbs be little Elizabeth in search of her body? Further investigations are needed.

Our Experiences and Opinions

We heard the story of the city gates on our ghost walk. It was quite interesting to hear about little Elizabeth, but there was something to think about. How many children would not be known to SOMEONE in town? Also, if nobody claimed her, how did they know her name was Elizabeth? I guess if you have to give the little girl a name,

Elizabeth would be just fine. As I write this, I wonder if someone caught her name in an EVP. That would be interesting to know for sure.

After the tour, Marianne and I went back to this location and took some photos. Marianne has a habit of taking a large quantity of photographs and that night she took several at the city gates. We were at the gate late into the night. This was well after our ghost tour was over and close to midnight. We remember that we kept asking Elizabeth to come out and dance with us. When we went back and looked at the photos years later, we did notice that we captured several orbs at this location. Several of them appeared on command when we asked them too. The more we asked the question, more and more orbs would appear in the photographs. We cannot wait to go back to this location with a recorder and try to capture little Elizabeth on an EVP.

Marianne with orbs around her.

As we continued to ask Elizabeth to come and dance with us, more orbs showed up in our photos. (You can see full color photos on PANICd.com)

7 CASTILLO DE SAN MARCOS

PANICd#: 1047

1 South Castillo Drive
St. Augustine, FL 32084

A Little History

Constructed between 1672 and 1695, the Castillo de San Marcos is the oldest fort in the United States. It was built by the Spanish as protection of the northernmost outpost in North America, St. Augustine. The outside walls of the fort are 30 feet high, average 12 feet thick, and made from about 400,000 locally mined coquina stone. The design of the outer walls of the fort were built at angles, both horizontally and vertically. This helped greatly with fortification since it was much harder to scale the walls with this design. Cannon and musket fire would ricochet off the sloped walls. This design with the hard coquina stone made the fort impregnable from attacks and was large enough to not only protect the military, but also the townspeople of St. Augustine.

Another feature of the fort was the moat built between the fort and the outer walls. Many believed for years that this was a water moat that they were to fill in case of attack. However, this proved to be incorrect. When the National Park Service took over the fort, they filled the moat with water and this started to cause damage to the fort walls. Once this was noticed, they immediately drained the moat. It is now believed that the moat was actually a dry moat. This was where they would store the animals during a siege of the town, thus separating the people from the animals for health reasons. There would sometimes be months where the townspeople would be held within the walls of the fort and this design proved to be quite handy to protect the animals as well.

After the U.S. acquired Florida and took over the fort, it became a military prison and renamed it Fort Marion. The Confederacy took control of the fort at the beginning of the Civil War without a fight. In March of 1862, the Union troops took back control of the fort and the town of St. Augustine without any shots being fired. The fort was retired from active status in 1899.

In 1924, the twenty five acre site was established as a National Monument. In 1942, the name of the fort was changed back to the Castillo de San Marcos in honor of its rich history. The fort is now managed by the National Park Service and can be visited every day with the exception of Christmas.

Ghostly Encounters, Stories, and/or Folklore

Although there are several reports of phenomena that take place in and around the grounds of the fort, there are two main stories that are associated with the site.

The first one is related to Colonel Garcia Marti, who was in charge of the Spanish military stationed at the fort. For almost a year, he heard rumors that one of his assistants, Captain Manuel Abela, was having an affair with his wife, Dolores Marti, yet, he could never prove that anything was going on between them. Captain Abela was described as being, "young, handsome, and charming."

Delores wore a perfume that was unique and sweet smelling. One day while Captain Abela was giving his report to Colonel Marti, the colonel recognized the smell of his wife's perfume on the Captain's uniform. In the darkness of night, when most of the soldiers had gone back to town to spend the night, both Dolores and Captain Abela disappeared. When the soldiers began inquiring as to where Captain Abela was, Colonel Marti told the soldiers that Captain Abela was sent on a special mission to Cuba.

Dolores' friends began to wonder what happened to her too. Colonel Marti told them, with great concern, that Dolores had become ill due to the weather in St. Augustine and was sent to live with her Aunt in Mexico who would nurse her back to health. Eventually he suggested that Dolores was sent to Spain to live. Her friends were not so sure though. She had not appeared ill. Questions and theories began about, but Colonel Marti's story was never directly challenged and it wasn't until almost 50 years later that the truth was discovered.

An American officer named Lieutenant Tuttle stationed at the fort in 1833. He was studying the architecture of the fort and was curious when he found an anomaly in one of the walls of the dungeon area. It appeared to be a void. After taking down the wall, he found a hidden room and the skeletal remains of two former prisoners chained to the wall. It is thought that Captain Marti had Dolores and Captain Abela chained up and left for dead. Presumably, some of the guards on duty were in cahoots with the colonel and which helped keep this revenge went undiscovered until Lt. Tuttle found the hidden room.

The next story related to the North Tower. This tower was often lit by candles and lamps by the soldiers who were on duty during the night hours. Today, there is no light in the North Tower. Yet, there have been many reports that when there is a storm and the seas are rough, there is a light that comes on in the tower. The light has been investigated on several occasions, but there was never anyone found in the tower. Could these soldiers still be on duty, helping to guide ships during dark or rough nights?

Paranormal Claims

- In the watch tower closest to the road, it is said that a light ignites on stormy nights. Residents and locals that are familiar with the fort often overlook this unexplained phenomenon, but for the avid ghost hunter, seeing this makes for a remarkable experience.
- People report seeing a soldier who is lavishly dressed in clothing of the Spanish era looking out at sea. This apparition is normally seen when the sun is just starting to rise or when the sun is setting.
- Many tourists have experienced strange sensations in the dungeon, including goose bumps, breezes, touches, and physical sickness for no apparent reason.

- Sounds of soldier's boots have been heard in the soldier's quarters by staff members.
- A staff member saw the indentation of a full form of a soldier lying in one of the beds in the soldier's quarters.
- People are sometimes shoved in the cannon room.
- An apparition of a soldier is sometimes seen walking along a wall of the castle, with a lantern.
- Footsteps of soldiers are sometimes heard running around the courtyard.
- An apparition of an executed English pirate has been seen at the wall where he died via a firing squad.
- The head of a Native American has been seen floating around the walls of the courtyard looking displeased.

Potential of Haunting

Many elements can be contributing to the haunting of this old fort. The fort is made of locally quarried coquina stone, which is made up of crushed shells and limestone. A well-known paranormal theory is that limestone can trap paranormal energy and be a potential cause of residual phenomena. The location of the fort is located on the banks of the Matanzas River, which flows into the ocean. Another paranormal theory is that flowing water can provide energy for spirits to manifest easier.

This is fort is now operated by the National Park Service who employs living history actors to reenact the life and times of soldiers in the fort when it was active. Almost on a daily basis there are men who are dressed in period clothing; reenacting, marching, and firing the cannons on the top of the fort. All of this can act as trigger events for spirits who may be trapped at the fort and not know that they have passed. They may notice these things going on and just think that it is still the time when they were alive and not a century or more later.

Lastly, we need to examine the tragic deaths at the fort. This would include the two lovers found chained up in the dungeon. Besides this story though, there were many other tragic or barbaric events that took place within the walls of the fort and when it served as a military prison. There is a paranormal theory that when there are tragic events that take place, negative energy can affect the area and cause residual phenomenon to occur within or around the area.

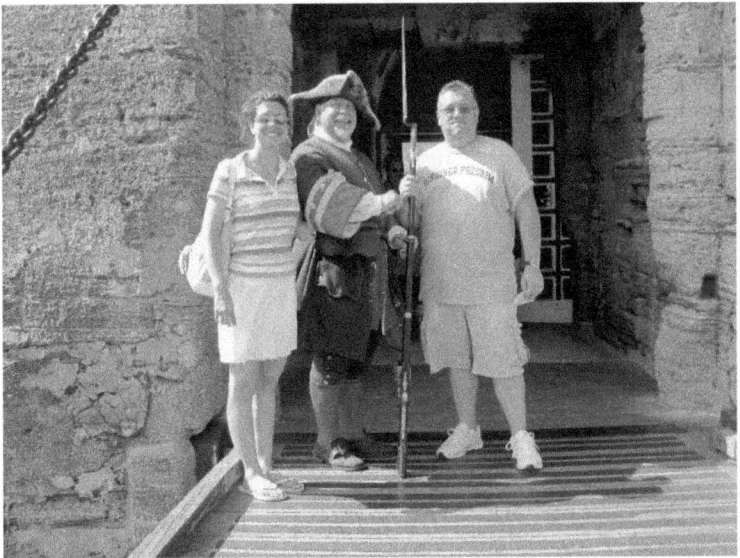

Our Experiences and Opinions

We have visited the Castillo de San Marcos a few times. You simply cannot visit St. Augustine without taking a tour inside. Unfortunately, since it is operated by the National Park Service, we have never had the privilege of going inside at night when it was closed. Marianne did however, get the chance to crawl through the opening in the wall and went back into the dungeon. She has pictures taken back there showing the chains they found on the wall.

We aren't sure there is option of visiting the place when it is closed, unless you have a major television production company backing you, but this would be an awesome place to perform a paranormal investigation. The expanse of the facility is amazing and there are multiple levels. We have been outside the fort at night during our ghost walk. We have also taken pictures of the fort in the evenings where we captured an orb on one of the walls.

We would love to have this place just to ourselves at night for a full investigation, even if for a few hours. Not that we believe that spirits only come out at night. Just as so many other investigators would also indicate, so we know that no other visitors are in the fort while conducting our investigation to contaminate our evidence.

The last time that we visited, they fired one of the cannons from the top of the fort. They do this almost daily, but it is impressive to be standing close them when the cannon goes off. A group of men dressed in period clothing line up on command downstairs in the main parade area. They then march up the steps and over to one of the cannons. As the orders go out, the military men go through the proper motions of loading the cannon and preparing it to fire. With everyone standing around in great anticipation, the commander yells, "FIRE!" They light the fuse of the cannon and the boom echoes all around the fort. They fire bread out into the bay for the wildlife to eat. What a great bird feeder and an awesome trigger object. No pun intended. It's a pretty awesome experience and they definitely take you back in time.

The next time we visit, we will be going on tour with our recorders rolling. Marianne definitely wants to visit the dungeon room and try to communicate with Dolores and Captain Abela.

8 AVILES STREET

PANICd#: 1013

Aviles Street
St. Augustine, FL 32084

A Little History

Aviles Street in the historic district of St. Augustine, Florida has long been identified as the oldest street in the United States. In the summer of 2010, this was authenticated by archaeologists. The city planners decided to replace the brick street and water lines in hopes to bring the road up to modern standards which would allow for easier maintenance. When digging began, it was discovered that there were many treasures hidden underneath the brick road. The project commissioned by the city had the street dug up in two test sections. During this excavation, bones from human limbs and pottery from the 1600's were found over a meter below the current brick road. This ended the upgrade project of the city and they replaced everything, including the original brick road.

The street was originally called Hospital Street since the hospital was located along this street, but it was eventually renamed in honor of the hometown of the city's founder. The bricks on the road are imprinted with "Reynolds Block", the name of the company who made the bricks.

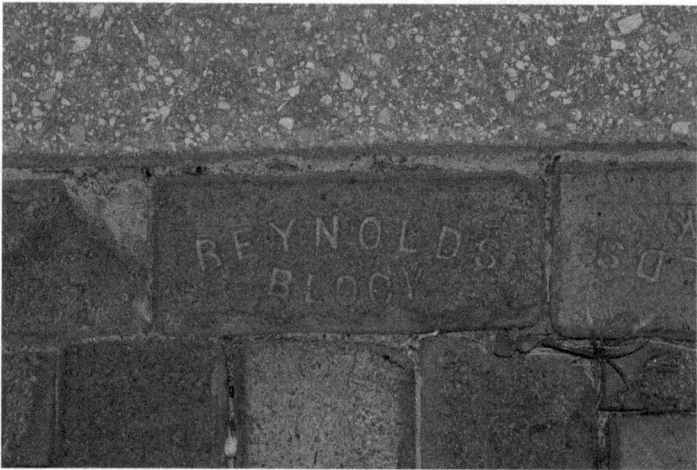

Ghostly Encounters, Stories, and/or Folklore

The street runs past the front of the St. Augustine Spanish Military Hospital, so most of the stories that we have heard about relating to Aviles Street are related to the hospital. There are a couple of stories that expand upon about Aviles Street itself.

Bodies and body parts were under the ground in front of the Spanish Military Hospital since before Aviles Street was formally made into a road. The section of the road towards the front or entrance of the street was an alley that ran between two medical buildings that were part of the hospital. After surgeons would remove body parts from the patients, they were buried in this alley. Over a period of time, the area became a mass "body part" grave. One could imagine how this practice would escalate during or after periods of battle that took place within the city.

The next story that we have is related to Henry Flagler and the Reynolds bricks that you see on Aviles Street and through the streets that are still paved with bricks within the historical district of St. Augustine. The streets were laid with bricks so that Henry Flagler's guests at his hotel would not have to walk on the dirt roads and get dirty as they strolled around the historical district. The story goes that there was some sort of dispute between Flagler and Reynolds over the price per brick and Flagler got the better end of the deal financially. Since Reynolds was not happy with his business dealings with Flagler, he made sure that all the bricks were stamped with the words "Reynolds Block" so that Flagler's upper class guests would see his name all the way to the Flagler hotel. Flagler was often reminded of the dealings when his guests would ask about Reynolds's name on the bricks.

Paranormal Claims

- Numerous orbs are seen along the street.

Potential of Haunting

We believe that the phenomenon happening on the street is probably associated with the Spanish Military Hospital. These entities may be outside the confines of the building, but instead confined to the street due to the variety of body parts and maybe even full unclaimed bodies that were buried under the road. The entire area of the historical section has paranormal claims, but Aviles Street has some activity that just cannot be explained.

Our Experiences and Opinions

We include this street for one reason. This is the street where we experienced our first paranormal occurrence. If you have read the previous chapters, you know that we went on a walking ghost tour that began at the Spanish Military Hospital. After the tour, we stopped by the Tolomato Cemetery, then headed across town to our bed and breakfast. The path we decided to take was past the Spanish Military Hospital down Aviles Street.

As we passed the hospital, Marianne was taking pictures as we walked. She continued to turn around taking photos as we went farther down the street. At one point she showed me the camera and said, "Wow! That is weird."

In the photos, it appeared that we had a group of orbs following us down the street. We thought this was some kind of smudge on the camera lens though since the orbs were appearing in different sizes and at different places on the photograph that was unlikely. In addition, they held the same texture and color. Was this one of the spirits that we encountered on the tour or was this something that was originating from Aviles Street itself? Once we left that street and turned the corner, the orbs stopped following us and did not appear in additional pictures; as if they had to stay on Aviles Street.

Most paranormal investigators or researchers will dismiss orbs in photographs because there are too many things that can cause them to occur such as dust, bugs, or even moisture in the air. We are extreme skeptics when it comes to evidence, and we spent many hours looking over these photos. If you flip through them in sequence, you can almost identify a path that the orbs took while they were following us and we discounted any photos that could have had a glare coming from some kind of reflective surface. You can view these photos in color on the PANICd.com website in the evidence section. Again, we cannot wait to go back in order to try and duplicate the phenomenon we experienced.

Photos taken on Aviles Street (see full sized color photos on PANICd.com)

9 OLD ST. JOHN'S JAIL

PANICd#: 1528

167 San Marco Avenue
St. Augustine, FL 32084

A Little History

The history of this building correlates to the building of
the Ponce de Leon Hotel by Henry Flagler. Flagler wanted
to ensure a safe, pleasant environment for his patrons by
creating a secure fortress to house criminals. The original
St. Augustine jail was originally located too close to the
town center for Flagler's liking, so he asked that the new
jail be built further out of town. He actually paid the
county $10,000 for the move. It was also extremely
important that the exterior of the building would not
disrupt the atmosphere of the city. In order to accomplish

this, the new jail was designed with a Romanesque Revival style that gave the distinct appearance of a Victorian house although it was missing the interior comfort and charm. As people would travel past the building, it was almost unrecognizable as a jail. The only thing that gave it away were the bars on the windows.

The P.J. Pauley Jail Company, that built Alcatraz in San Francisco, was contracted to construct the new prison. The jail served the city of St. Augustine until 1963 and it held some of the most violent and sadistic criminals. The jail even carried out capital punishment on a set of gallows for those who were sentenced to death.

The philosophy of jails at the time was that prisoners were there to be punished, not rehabilitated. Therefore, the conditions at the jail were considered to be horrible at best. The food served was grits for breakfast, hard tac if the prisoners were sent out to work, and beans for dinner. Blankets and pillows were considered to be a luxurious option and the beds were made of Spanish moss, a breeding ground for bugs. There were also no bathing options.

The prisoners were not protected from the whims of the guards, the sheriff, or the warden. Solitary confinement and other overly harsh punishments were dished out for minor offenses. The solitary confinement area had no windows and no bed and prisoners could sometimes spend months in these rooms.

The windows of the jail had no glass, just bars. The building was built with no heat, no running water, and no sanitation for the disposal of human waste. There was only one bucket provided for every four prisoners. The building would become extremely cold in the winters and the summer months would sometimes become unbearable with heat. Sick prisoners were kept among the general population, often times spreading more sickness to the other prisoners. Many prisoners would pass away from sickness with no medical treatment.

The one thing that kept the prisoners from going insane was the work program. This program brought the prisoners outside the walls of the building and put them to work in the surrounding community. Although they were working long hours and the conditions were terrible, this allowed the prisoners an opportunity to catch small animals to help supplement their less than healthy diets. If they got an opportunity to escape, they found that the public would help them. The general population of the town knew about and did not approve of the abusive conditions in the jail.

Ghostly Encounters, Stories, and/or Folklore

Most places with reported paranormal claims have claims in reference to cold spots or unpredictable breezes. Most investigators and researchers believe that these are intelligent entities trying to manifest and the exchange of energy is causing the cold spot. Many visitors have reported feeling these strange cold spots, feeling cold hands touching their shoulder or tugging their hair, and feeling someone blowing on them as they walk by a cell.

Strange moaning and crying sounds have been reported coming from the maximum security and solitary confinement areas. Some visitors have also reported hearing the voice of a little girl in the sheriff's quarters. Others have heard someone whistling at them. Several visitors have even reported hearing a dastardly laugh in one of the women's cells.

The building is cleaned daily, however, there are occasions when weird aromas are detected. One of these is the smell of sewage in the air, although there is none to be found on the site. Others report a sickeningly sweet smell, which many describe as the smell of molasses boiling on a stove top. Again, after investigation and looking for the source of the smell, none can be found.

Today, the location is a museum with no one living on the premises. There are occasions when visitors have heard a dog barking inside, but employees guarantee that there are no dogs currently located in the building. When the jail was open, the sheriff and his family lived there and the family did have pet dogs.

Many people who live close to the old jail frequently report the frequent sounds of footsteps walking inside the jail late at night after it has closed. They report loud, clunky noises like someone wearing chains moving around inside as well. These sounds have also been reported by those who visit the jail during the daytime.

Paranormal Claims

- At random times, the smell of sewage and a sickeningly sweet smell of molasses have been reported.
- An apparition of a man was seen sitting on a chair.
- A cowering apparition was spotted in a cell by a tour guide, but disappeared through a wall.
- Unseen presences are felt by the living; they tug at, blow on, and talk or whistle to those folks who come inside the building.
- A male presence was sensed by a psychic, pacing

the hallway by the kitchen.

- In one of the women's cells, a very grumpy unseen presence has been known to push and trip people.
- During a tour, a tour guide felt a punch in his side and a cold hand move down his back.
- A psychic medium found an entity that had been seen around the building. She found out that this entity was executed by hanging for a crime he didn't commit and was afraid to go to the light because of other misdeeds.
- Voices of unseen presences wailing, yelling, and moaning have been heard directly by the living.
- An EVP of a nasty laugh was heard by a man opening the safe in the office.
- The sound of a little girl's voice has been heard in one of the children's bedrooms used by the sheriff warden's family.
- Shuffling footsteps and the jingling of chains are heard around and on the steps of the jail.
- Neighbors heard disembodied barking of dogs coming from the back of the jail where the prison dogs were kept.

Potential of Haunting

It is not surprising that this old jail is haunted. Most locations that house the incarcerated are a magnet for paranormal activity. There tend to be both residual and intelligent haunting in locations like this and this location is no different. There are several reports of inmates dying from disease, abuse, and attacks by other inmates. There are even reports of a sheriff's daughter dying either from disease or an accidental death. Sudden, accidental, or premature deaths can cause entities to remain at the location where their human existence ceased.

Just outside the building in the courtyard of this location is a gallows that was used for multiple executions as well. These executions were not often quick and were extremely painful. It is possible that the spirits of these prisoners did not want to cross or feared crossing over since they felt guilty of their crimes and were afraid of their own judgment.

Our Experiences and Opinions

We had the opportunity to visit the jail on the day tour. I remember having an eerie feeling as I walked through the halls and visited the cells. The building today is extremely clean and very well preserved, but when you approach the back of the building and look out you can see the gallows. They make you remember that the building was a jail and many former inmates lost their lives in that location.

When we were there we were not aware of the paranormal activity that was reported. We found this out later when we researched the location for PANICd.com. We even went back and looked through all of our photos from this location, but did not see anything paranormal. We definitely have to go back with a recorder and the knowledge of what we have now in hopes of capturing an EVP or two.

10 BAYFRONT MARIN HOUSE

PANICd#: 1891

142 Avenida Menendez
St. Augustine , FL 32084

A Little History

According the location's website, the first recorded history of the property that the Bayfront Marin house now resides is from a Roque map from 1788 that shows a wooden building in bad condition.   Franciso Marin who was a member of the Minorcan colony obtained the house and lot in the 1780's and Francisco Marin, Jr., was granted the title by Governor White in 1806.

Today the Bayfront Marin House is actually made up of multiple buildings that were located on the property and adjoining properties that were brought together to create the large beautiful building that is standing at this time.

The rear section of the building contains the colonial house on Marine Street which dates back to the Second Spanish Period. This section is built right to the street line, with the walls extending north and south from the facade and no door facing the street. This style shows the effects of the early regulations laid out by the royal ordinance issued by the King of Spain in 1573 indicating that:

> "All town houses are to be so planned that they can serve as a defense or fortress against those who might attempt to create disturbances or occupy the town."

Today the building owes its structure mainly to Captain Henry Belknap who originally came to St. Augustine as a guest of the Alcazar. During his stay, decided to purchase property for himself. He purchased a Victorian Cottage that stood on Bay Street (which is now Avenida Mendendez). North of the Marin house was another property owned by Andrew Burgess. Captain Belknap purchased this property as well in 1893. After his second purchase, he moved the Burgess cottage and attached it to the back of his other cottage. Soon he also purchased the Marin house and began to make wooden additions to the coquina building. When finished, three houses were combined to make the current structure. The structure then had a wide range of structural components spanning from the colonial period all through the ornate Flagler era.

After the death of Captain Henry in 1909, the building had various owners (including John Cambell, Beulah Robinson Lewis, Graubard, and Stacklum) who converted the building into apartments and short-term rental units throughout the years.

In 2003, the house was converted into the Bayfront Marin House and it is now a bed and breakfast with rooms named for some individuals who had great influence on it throughout history.

Ghostly Encounters, Stories, and/or Folklore

We found two stories for this location. The first talks about a guest complaining to the innkeepers that the people who were staying above him were having a very loud party in the middle of the night. He stated that around 2:00 AM, the room above became so loud with their partying that he got out of bed and travelled up the steps to pound on the door in order to get them to stop. Nobody answered the door, but the noise stopped so, he went back down stairs and climbed back in bed. About half an hour later, the noise became so loud again that he had to go back upstairs, this time he threatened to call the authorities if they did not stop. Immediately, the noise stopped, but again nobody answered the door. They were quiet for the rest of the night.

The next morning, he complained to the innkeepers and was surprised when he was told that there was nobody staying above him and his wife. Nobody had rented the room the previous evening. He did not believe them and said they were partying so hard the room had to be trashed. The innkeeper took him upstairs to show him that the room was cleaned and undisturbed as the cleaning staff left it several days before.

Another story involved when the inn had to get a repairman out to look at one of the phone lines in a room that was not working. The man that came out was an expert with thirty-four years of experience in the telephone business. He determined that the line was dead at the street, but when he picked up the phone he could hear a music playing that only came from the receiver. When asked if in all his years of experience, he had ever ran into that phenomenon in St. Augustine, he replied, "more than you can imagine."

Paranormal Claims

- Parties have been heard on the second floor late into the night when nobody is checked into the room.
- Music has been heard on dead telephone lines.

Potential of Haunting

There are a few reasons why we believe that this location can have a potential haunting. We don't believe that they are residual since the claims that we have found state that they only happen occasionally. There is a paranormal theory that states that entities sometime come back and visit places that they enjoyed during life. The story that we found states that they believe it is Francisco Marin coming back to have some fun, but we don't think that would be true. If anyone would be coming back to have fun it would be Captain Henry. As the history states, he loved St. Augustine and purchased the property to make it his home. It is possible he used to have parties or host guests on occasion, which would explain the one story. Could he be coming back to the home he loved to have a party?

Another paranormal theory is that entities can draw their energy from water. There is a large body of water, right across the street from this house.

Lastly, between the time of being a home for Captain Henry and now, this location has seen a lot of visitors. It was an apartment building, short-term rooms, and now a bed and breakfast. Another paranormal theory states that many different people at a location can leave segments of energy behind for other entities to draw power on to manifest. This may apply here.

Our Experiences and Opinions

We mentioned in the other chapters about our bed and breakfast and this was the location we stayed at in 2010. It was one of our first bed and breakfast experiences. It was a beautiful place to stay and spend some relaxing time. I wish I could say we had a paranormal experience while staying here, but to be honest we didn't. At least we don't know if we did or not. They were setting up for and event. We could see it from our room. We really did not notice any partying…but we did go out on the ghost tour that night and may have missed it. We would definitely stay at this location in the future and may even have a chance to run into Francisco Marin or Captain Henry.

If you are traveling to St. Augustine, we highly suggest you look into staying here. It was a pleasant atmosphere in which to start your day out on the patio having breakfast or to end your day sitting out on the patio gazing at the bay and the stars.

11 HUGUENOT CEMETERY

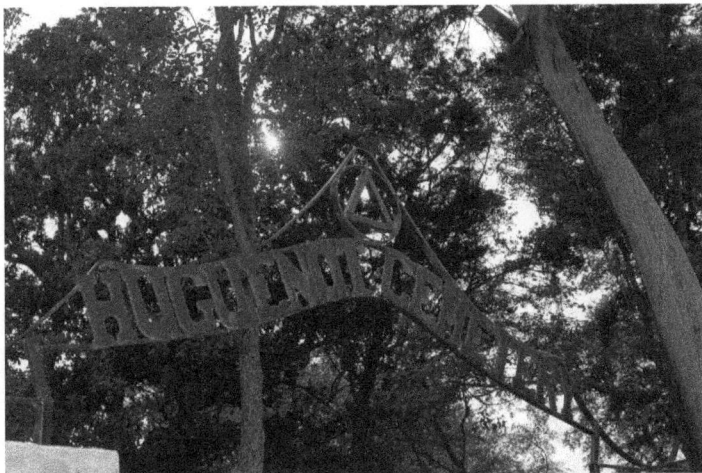

PANICd#: 1896

A1A Orange St
St. Augustine, FL 32084

A Little History

The Huguenot Cemetery is located directly across from the Old City Gates. This cemetery was the town's burial ground between the years 1821 and 1884 for non-catholics. (The town's Catholic cemetery was the Tolomato cemetery.)

The first burials in the cemetery occurred in 1821. While city records show that there are at least 436 burials within the cemetery, there are also records of mass graves due to the yellow fever outbreak which reduced the city's population by very great numbers within a very short time period.

The name of the cemetery is Huguenot Cemetery, but it is believed that there are actually no members of the Huguenots buried within the grounds.

Ghostly Encounters, Stories, and/or Folklore

Some of the St. Augustinians refer to the cemetery as "Spirit Central" because of the large amount of paranormal activity reported about this site. There are hundreds of stories and claims related to this cemetery including hearing male laughter, crackling of leaves without winds or passers by, multitudes of orbs, mists, and strange flashes of light --all which go unexplained. There are two stories though that are very well known amongst the citizens of St. Augustine.

First, do you remember the story from the Old City Gates about the little girl named Elizabeth? She is also reportedly seen on the grounds of this cemetery. She is believed to be buried in one of the yellow fever mass graves here in Huguenot Cemetery. Reports have been made of her playing around the trees waving at visitors to the cemetery. She reportedly wears a flowing white gown and is most often seen between midnight and 2 a.m.

The next story relates to Judge John Stickney. The story goes that the Judge's wife had previously passed away, leaving him to raise his young children himself. When the judge passed away in 1882, this left his children orphans. The children were sent to family members up north. Their father's grave however, was in St. Augustine. Once the children had grown, they decided to exhume and re-inter their father's body in Washington, D.C. near where they resided.

During the exhumation process, the gravediggers took a short break to get some refreshments and left the casket unattended in an open grave. When they returned from their break, they found that thieves had stolen the Judge's gold teeth. Noticing what had happened, they quickly closed up the coffin so that nobody would discover the missing teeth. There was apparently only one issue. The judge seemed to have noticed. Since the exhumation and theft, there have been reports of a tall dark figure, who roams the cemetery as if looking for someone or something. It is thought that this could be the judge looking for those who stole his teeth or even perhaps for the teeth themselves.

Paranormal Claims

- The apparition of a young girl dressed in white has been seen dancing around the graves and trees; waving at visitors.
- The apparition of a man, thought to be Judge Stickney, has been seen roaming around the cemetery looking for something.
- Orbs have been captured in photographs.
- Shadows and strange mists have been captured in photographs.
- People have heard the sound of a man laughing.
- People have heard the sounds of leaves crackling and bushes moving with nothing there to make the noises.

Potential of Haunting

Contrary to most beliefs, cemeteries and graveyards are not normally places for paranormal activity. In fact, cemeteries should be places where you would not experience paranormal activity. These are meant to be final, peaceful resting places for our bodies after we pass onto the other side.

However, it is also believed that cemeteries gain a reputation for being haunted for reasons that include the desecration of the dead, grave robbery, unmarked or forgotten graves, natural disasters that disturb resting places, or improper burials. It is believed that those who are in one of these circumstances come back to find out why and/or try to fix their situation.

Our Experiences and Opinions

Before we had our experiences at Tolomato Cemetery, we stopped at the Huguenot Cemetery a few times and I must admit it is one of the spookiest looking cemeteries we have ever seen. Even during the day time, this cemetery looks like something straight out of the writings of Edgar Allan Poe. With crypts above ground and remnants of Victorian Era burials, you sure do get the feeling of a ghostly presence when you are there. You do not have to go into this cemetery to view some of the burials, since the fence is low and you are able to walk around the entire perimeter.

Our plans when we go back to this location are to definitely bring the Ovilus (an ITC device used for spirit communications) and a recorder. We tend to have good luck with using the Ovilus in cemeteries. We are certain we will capture some great evidence within this cemetery.

Although we took several pictures in and around the cemetery, there was nothing that we determined to be strange or paranormal on our visit. Most of our photos were taken during a day visit. We need to spend more time at this location both during the day and at night.

12 O.C. WHITE'S SEAFOOD AND SPIRITS

PANICd#: 1526

118 Avenida Menendez
St. Augustine, FL 32084

A Little History

This building dates back to 1790. The structure was built by Don Miguel YsNardy, as a private residence between 1791 and 1799. At one time, this house served as one of St. Augustine's first hotels. Throughout the years it was names, The Union Hotel, Levington's, and Bridier's. It was eventually bought by the Worth family in the 1850s and converted back to a private home. It remained as a private residence for many generations. In 1904, the Worth Mansion was bought by a local cigar maker. In 1917, the building was used as the Chamber of Commerce headquarters. In 1924, the building was a tourist club and apartment building, then in 1948 it was purchased by George L. Potter, the onetime owner of Potter's Wax Museum. In 1961, the building was demolished and moved to its present location (using the original materials) from across the street. In the early 1990s, businessman Dave White bought the Worth Mansion in hope of opening a pub and restaurant.. Although the exterior of the building now replicates the Worth House as it appeared in the mid-nineteenth century, there were extensive modifications inside to better suit the needs of a restaurant rather than a private residence. It is now a restaurant named O.C. White's Seafood and Spirits.

During the renovations of the building, right before the opening of the restaurant, there was a mysterious fire that originated in a waiter's storage closet. This fire caused damage to the second and third floors and blew out the windows. The interesting part of this was there was nothing flammable or combustible stored within this closet at the time. The investigation of the fire could not find the source.

The current building is three stories, built from coquina bricks, with hardwood floors and mid-nineteenth century windows throughout. As patrons enter, there are tables on the left and a little wooden bar on the right. The kitchen is located off the main room. There is also a large dining room is located off the main room. There is a central staircase leading up to the second floor, where the bedrooms were located when it was a private residence. These bedrooms have been converted to now be an open dining room. The second floor has a stairway leading to the third floor where the offices are located today.

Ghostly Encounters, Stories, and/or Folklore

Most of the paranormal activity in the building seems to be related to the Worth family. The Worth family purchased the building which was a hotel in the early 1850s and converted it into a family home. Mrs. Margaret Worth was the widow of a distinguished war hero named General William Jenkins Worth, the man whom Fort Worth, Texas is named after. (The Worth family was originally from New York, but General Worth was stationed in Florida before he was transferred to Texas.) When she purchased the home, she did some renovations to convert it back to being a private home, modernizing it to fit into the architecture of the time.

Margaret loved her new home and she lived there by herself for some time until after the Civil War, when her daughter and son-in-law, Colonel John T. Sprague, moved in with her. The couple lived with Mrs. Worth until she died in 1869, but the mansion remained in the family until 1904.

This history relates to a story about the current owner, Dave "OC" White. One day he was washing his hands in the men's bathroom and he looked up in the mirror to see a man standing behind him with a tall top hat. Mr. White excused himself to get out of the way, but when he turned around the man had vanished. Several years later, he was shown a historical picture and explained that that the man in the photograph was the one whom he saw in the mirror years previously. The man in the photograph was Colonel John T. Sprague.

Paranormal Claims

- Though the owner's third floor office looked like charcoal after a fire, a picture of the original Worth Mansion and an elaborate light fixture were completely untouched, as if something had protected them.
- While boarding up a window from the inside, the owner heard the loud voice of an unseen upset female presence in close proximity.
- In the third floor office, an unseen male presence makes his presence known by his ripe aroma.
- In the third floor office, sometimes when they are about to unlock the office, the door suddenly opens up by itself by a helpful entity, thought to be Mrs. Worth.
- After locking the door to the third floor office, and going downstairs, staff have heard that same door slam shut.
- In the third floor office, keys left on the office desk have been known to disappear, but then reappear in an hour or so.
- While in the third floor office, closing up for the night, the owner and others occasionally hear footsteps walking around the second floor that then proceed to come up the stairs to the office. There is no one there.
- Two patrons and three waiters in the second floor dining area watched as two salt shakers moved around the table several times.
- All the table candles are always blown out during the closing routine. Sometimes all the candles are found lit on the tables upstairs.
- Clothes and purses are moved around by unseen energy throughout the building.

- Beads left hanging on wall decorations move to other locations.
- A waiter was once coming down the stairs with some trays when she was "zapped" in the stomach by a shock, like from a buzzer, causing much alarm.
- In the kitchen, pots and pans move on their own.

Potential of Haunting

We have five potential contributors to paranormal activity at this location that need to be mentioned. First, let's discuss the theory of renovation. The paranormal theory related to renovation is that there is heightened paranormal activity that takes place when a building is renovated. This building has been renovated several times. It was converted from a personal home to other types of businesses including hotels, back to looking like the original home again with some modifications for modern times. Now it is a restaurant. It is possible that the spirit of Mrs. Worth was coming back to help out, overseeing the renovations.

Second, we want to discuss the building being a hotel and restaurant. Notoriously, there is paranormal activity reported at hotels. There are two theories that can be explained about this; high traffic in the building and high levels of positive or negative energy from multiple sources. When you have several individuals within a building over time, this energy can leave an imprint on the location and cause residual paranormal activity. Countless hotels and restaurants have been associated with paranormal entities that that do not seem to want to leave. Some of these are known to be pranksters which could account for the moving of items or missing items. Others may be former employees just continuing to perform daily tasks – like the lighting of candles and opening doors.

Third, the materials used to build the building. This building is made from coquina stone. Coquina stone is a locally quarried stone in St. Augustine, but it contains high levels of limestone. Limestone is known to trap energy and can contribute to paranormal activity.

Fourth, the former mansion. It is documented that Mrs. Worth loved her home. She had it renovated to suit her needs and she lived out the remainder of her life at the location. There is a paranormal theory that a soul can become attached to an earthy location or item and sometimes come back to visit that location that they loved when they were here on earth.

Fifth, the water. This location sits on the bay of the Matanzas River. There is a paranormal theory that flowing water can provide energy for spirits to use in order to create paranormal activity, both residual and intelligent. St. Augustine is surrounded by flowing water.

Our Experiences and Opinions

We walked past this location every night as we traveled back to our bed and breakfast for the evening. We stopped once for dinner, but sat outside. We should've known the place had spirits other than those that you drink, since most of the buildings in St. Augustine have an interesting history and potential for paranormal activity. We were not aware the last time that this was the case since our investigating and research did not begin until a later date. This location is definitely on the list for a future visit. We intend to make to have a table inside this time.

13 HARRY'S SEAFOOD BAR AND GRILLE

PANICd#: 1892

46 Avenida Menendez
St. Augustine, FL 32084

A Little History

This building was originally built sometime around 1745 out of "tabby" or crushed oyster shells in plaster. According to records in the St. Augustine Historical Society, early owners were Francisco and Juana de Porras. The couple had nine children with the youngest named Catalina. Her family fled to Cuba when St. Augustine became a British Colony in 1763. In 1770, when Catalina was around eighteen years old, she married Xavier Ponce de Leon. In 1793, when the Spanish regained control of

Florida from the British, Catalina and her husband returned to St. Augustine to find that the house where she spent the first 10 years of her life had been used as a British storage barn. Catalina and her husband petitioned the governor to return the house to her and she regained ownership in 1789. Catalina's enjoyment of the home was short lived, since she died in 1795.

Not much else is known about the building (except that it changed hands several times) until 1887 when the house was destroyed by a fire that swept through a portion of St. Augustine. In 1888, it was rebuilt based on drawings of the house from 1840. The building sits on the original foundation, but unlike the original building, it now is made of concrete walls. The drawings used in the rebuild are what the house looked like at the time when Catalina owned the property.

Since the rebuild, the building has had yet again several different owners including one of Henry Flagler's descendants and the owner of "The Alligator Farm". At sometime after 1976 it was converted into a restaurant. There have been at four different restaurants since then at the location – Puerta Verde, the Chart House, Catalina's Gardens, and Harry's. It was in 1997, current owners opened up Harry's Seafood Bar and Grill and the restaurant is still there today.

As a side note, who is Harry of Hooked on Harry's? Well, Harry is the name of a long-shot horse. The owners wanted to open a restaurant based on Cajun restaurants they enjoyed in New Orleans, but they only had one problem; no funding. So they went to the horse races and put their money on a long shot. At 50-1, Harry the horse won. So the owners took their winnings and started their chain of restaurants called Harry's.

Ghostly Encounters, Stories, and/or Folklore

There are reports of at least two different spirits within this building, but possibly three. One is a woman in a wedding dress who has been seen around the patio area and around the upstairs woman's bathroom, which was believed to be Catlina's bedroom. Some have claimed to see this woman appear quickly then vanish into a wall or closed door. There are also reports of a drifting aroma of cheap perfume which is credited to this spirit as well. It is also reported that an entity in the upstairs ladies room will turn the water to scalding hot if she does not like you or thinks you are being rude.

The other spirit often reported in the building is that of a man in a black suit and hat. He has been frequently seen throughout the entire building on all three floors.

It is not specifically known who these spirits are and we were not able to find any records of paranormal investigations within the building. Past owners and employees acknowledge the unexplained events though. These could be the spirits of Catalina and her husband. Some believe that the woman could be someone named Bridget who supposedly died within the building. Who is the man? The man could be Calalina's husband or one of two different men who reportedly died in the building. One of the men died during the 1887 fire and the other succumbed to an illness around 1900.

Either way, the ghosts of the building do not seem to be conducting any major mischief or causing harm to the guests and employees of the current establishment. They seem to be mostly pleasant and friendly.

Paranormal Claims

- An apparition of a woman wearing a wedding dress has been reported being seen throughout the building and on the patio.
- An apparition of a man in a black suit has been seen throughout the building.
- The smell of women's perfume has been reported throughout the building.
- There have been reports of the water in the woman's bathroom turning on by itself.
- Reports of water in the upstairs ladies room turning to scalding hot.

Potential of Haunting

When thinking about what could be causing the paranormal activity of this location, the first thing that comes to mind is the theory related to the location being a formal home. Spirits can have a tendency to be attracted to locations and objects that brought them enjoyment when they were on earth and the theory is that they often come back to the location to visit. Since this location has had so many different tenants over the years, it is possible that one of more of them became attached to the location where they experienced joy during their short time on earth.

Another explanation can be the restaurant traffic. It would be hard to calculate how many people have entered the doors of this location over the years. With that many people passing through the location, if there are entities there, they have a renewable resource of energy to draw upon.

Another explanation, at least lending to the reports of the spirit of the man, (and maybe "Bridgett") is that of sudden and tragic deaths. If there was someone who died within the fire, they may not realize that they have passed and could be trapped at the location.

A final reasoning is of course again the water. This building sits along the waterfront on Avenida Menendez and of course water allows for entities to draw energy for manifestations.

Our Experiences and Opinions

We love this restaurant and ate out on the patio on many occasions. The food is great, the atmosphere is pleasant, and it is right off the bay on the main street. It has a tendency to get crowded for dinner, so make sure you either eat early or plan to wait as they do not take reservations. It is worth it though. The food is awesome.

As for paranormal experiences, we were not even aware this location had claims until we started researching for this book. We did not notice anything in particular to be paranormal, but we did feel a happy pleasant vibe in the patio area and have always requested to sit there on all of our subsequent dining experiences. Next time, Marianne will have to go and do an EVP session up in the women's restroom. We will also be sure to be a little more aware of our surroundings and maybe we will see Catalina or Bridgett—and maybe even the man in black. Maybe they will even sit down and dine with us.

14 OLD DRUG STORE

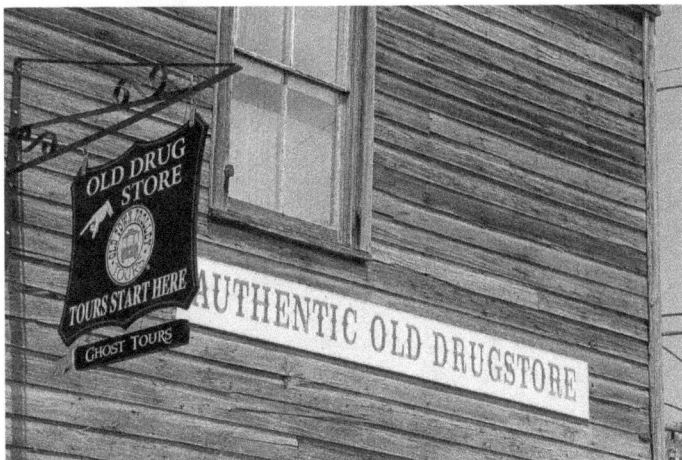

PANICd#: 1893

31 Orange St
St. Augustine, FL 32084

A Little History

A man by the name of Antonio Gomaas built this the original drugstore in 1739. He sold liquor, tobacco, medicine and many local Indian remedies to the townspeople of St. Augustine. In 1880, pharmacist T.W. Speissegger purchased the drugstore from Gomaas' decedents and after the famous fire of 1880's, moved to the two story wood framed building in its current location on the corner of Orange St. where he sold his own medical concoctions for many years.

After the passing of Speissegger, the building went

through many family owners and many renovations over the years until the 1960's. In the late 1980's it was purchased by the Harris Foundation.

The Harris foundation made many repairs and opened a museum that was free of charge to the public. The gift shop of the museum is located in an area of the building that was previously a courtyard. The Authentic Old Drugstore was maintained and supported solely by the sales in the gift shop.

In 2013, the building was purchased by Historic Tours of America and conducted more renovations to the tune of $250,000. The new owners looked into why the location was not listed as a historic site. They found that it actually was, so they pushed to have a historical marker added to the property. On March 26, 2015, the historical marker was unveiled.

This location is a stop on evening ghost tours. The Potter's wax museum is now housed at the same property.

Ghostly Encounters, Stories, and/or Folklore

This building sits on the edge of the Tolomato Cemetery and is one of St. Augustine's most recognizable buildings. Cold spots, strange unexplained noises, and shadows have been reported, and there are hundreds of reported supernatural occurrences that have taken place within the building.

One of the popular stories on the ghost walks and tours is that the drug store was built over a Tolomato village and Chief Tolomato himself is buried directly under the building. Inside the drugstore you will find a tombstone that reads:

"NOTIS. This werry elaborte pile is ereckted in memery of Tolomato a Seminole Ingine cheef whoos wigwarm stuud on this spot and sirroundings. Wee cherris his memery as he was a good harted cheef. He wood knot take yoour skalp without you begged him to do so or pade him sum munny. He always akted more like a Christsun gentle man than a savage Ingine. Let him R.I.P."

This is a very interesting story. However, for this book, Marianne needed to have something to debunk and she did deeper research about the internment of Chief Tolomato. What she has uncovered is that the stories that are being told during the ghost tours do not have exact truth behind them.

It is possible that there are bodies buried under the drugstore, since it is on the border of the cemetery, but not that of the actual chief. The chief of the Tolomato tribe went by the Spanish, Christian name of Don Juanillo and it is documented that he was killed somewhere in Georgia. Furthermore, Marianne found a photograph of the same shrine that is in the drugstore from 1911 showing that it was located across the street from the drugstore.

It turns out that the original owners of the drugstore moved the shrine inside the drugstore and made up the story about Chief Tolomato being buried under the building in order to get more store traffic from tourists. It makes a great story, but unfortunately it is not true.

With this being said, this does not discount the paranormal activity that takes place within the building. There are spirits that reside here, just not that of the chief. Some have reported jars and coffee cups breaking on their own, strange smells, odd sounds, and even footsteps late into the night. Are these the spirits of other Tolomato Indian tribe members or someone else? Either way, the drugstore is definitely an interesting place to stop and visit.

Paranormal Claims

- Strange sounds have been reported when nobody is around.
- Strange smells have been reported.
- Orbs and balls of light have been recorded.
- Glasses, cups, and jars have broken on their own.
- People have reported cold spots.
- People have reported seeing shadows throughout the building.

Potential of Haunting

The first thing that comes to mind for the potential of paranormal activity at this location is the displacement of the Native American tribe that had a small village at this location. It is also possible that there could of been burials under the building as well, since there are no accurate records of the original allotment of land for the Tolomato Cemetery as the ownership of the cemetery switch hands many times. If there are bodies beneath the building without proper, marked internment, this lends itself to the same theory that relates to paranormal activities at cemeteries. The graves were disturbed and those spirits are now not at peace.

Another thing to point out is that during the early history of this location, they used to sell liquor and tobacco. This borders on something that sounds similar to the characteristics of a saloon. It is possible that soldiers would go here to get their supplies and or wind down after a long day at the fort and who knows what type of activity took place within the walls of the building.

Most recently, with the addition of the Potter's Wax Museum to the property, who knows what additional energies will be available?

Our Experiences and Opinions

We briefly went inside the Old Drugstore during our ghost tour. We were not in there for very long and we heard the story of Chief Tolomato. We took several pictures while inside, but were not able to capture anything. We were only in the building for a few minutes though and we definitely need to go back with a recorder and to take more pictures. We would like to spend sometime around the outside of the building as well to see if there are any intelligent responses to EVP questions considering the land it is built upon.

15 CASA MONICA HOTEL

PANICd#: 1894

95 Cordova St
St. Augustine, FL 32084

A Little History

Some people believe that Henry Flagler built the Casa Monica Hotel. He didn't. He sold the land on which it stands to Franklin Smith, an amateur architect from Boston, who built the building. The original Casa Monica Hotel opened on New Year's Day in 1888. Four months after the opening, Flagler purchase the Casa Monica and all of the contents from Smith for $325,000 and changed the name of the hotel to the Cordova. Smith sold the property due to financial woes related to the hotel. The hotel flourished under Flagler's management.

In 1902, a bridge was built that connected the Cordova and one of Flagler's other hotels in St. Augustine, the Hotel Alcazar, which is now known as the Lightner Museum. They the bridge connected the second floor the two buildings. When this occurred, the Cordova changed its name to the Alcazar Annex. A year later, it was announced that the two buildings had became one hotel and advertised it as the "enlarged and redecorated" Alcazar. For nearly thirty years, the hotel again flourished under Flagler's tutelage, but it officially closed in 1932 as it was unable to maintained after Flagler relinquished the property as a result of the depression era.

In 1945, the bridge between the two buildings was removed. St. Johns County Commission purchased the Cordova building in 1962 for $250,000 and converted the hotel into a courthouse which opened in May of 1968. It remained a courthouse until the late 1970s. Finally, in the mid-1990s, Richard C. Kessler of the Kessler Enterprise, Inc. purchased the building with the plans to restore the building back to a hotel. The hotel was officially reopened in 1999 and is now known as the Casa Monica Resort and Spa.

Ghostly Encounters, Stories, and/or Folklore

This location is a hotbed for paranormal activity. Strange and unexplainable events have been reported by numerous employees and guests. However, the owners do not admit or recognize that there is anything going on of a supernatural nature.

One of the stories that we found was about a young woman who was hired as a housekeeper. She heard about the paranormal claims, until she had an unexplainable experience of her own. While working on the fourth floor, she knocked on a door to alert guests of her presence and heard a voice respond to her from inside the room. When she walked inside, she found the room empty. Somehow this experience was too much for her and she quit and never returned to the hotel.

There are also stories of apparitions dressed in period clothing spotted in various places around the hotel. There are those who believe that these spirits date back to the early days of the Casa Monica Hotel based on their attire. Several guests have spotted a woman in an elegant white dress. Others saw men in morning coats or dapper suits wandering the halls. Occasionally, they are so detailed, that guests have thought they were hotel employees who were dressed up for a reenactment of some kind.

Most of the activity in this building is concentrated on or around the fourth floor. There are two rooms in particular that tend to have more paranormal activity than others, room 411 and room 511. Guests of room 411 sometimes see apparitions of men in old-fashioned clothing. They are generally seen standing in the room amidst a conversation. The men then just suddenly disappear from view. In room 511, it has been identified that there was a suicide. The suicide was discovered by employees after the guest did not check out at the appropriate time. The body was found hanging from the ceiling. Since then, guests have reported feeling icy winds moving through room 511, finding cold spots in certain places and hearing footsteps when they were are alone in the room.

There are also reports from housekeepers and others who detest cleaning rooms on the fourth floor because of the things experiences that they have. Dozens of maids have reported hearing kids running, playing, and laughing in the hallway when they were inside the rooms cleaning. When check to see what all of the commotion was, there was nobody in the hallway. Others have encountered radios, alarm clocks, and sink faucets that come on in empty rooms. The stories and experiences are so common that the housekeeping department now permits maids to work together to clean the rooms on this floor.

Paranormal Claims

- In room 511, guests have reported icy winds moving throughout the room and cold spots.
- In room 511, guests have reported hearing footsteps when nobody else is in the room.
- In room 411, guests have reported seeing men in period clothing, then they disappear.
- People in period clothing have been seen throughout the building. Almost to a point where guests believe that they are employees dressed up as actors.
- One guest had a conversation with a women dressed in period clothes. She told him that she was present when they broke ground for the hotel.
- Children have been heard running in the hallways when nobody was present.
- Radios, alarm clocks, and faucets come on by themselves in empty rooms.
- Footprints have been found in the carpet of empty rooms.
- Lights turn on and off on their own.
- Doors lock and unlock on their own.
- People have reported the sounds of people whispering in the hallways.

Potential of Haunting

In reviewing the information for this location, it seems as if there is a lot of residual activity taking place. However, when you look at water, lights, or electronics turning on and off by themselves, and conversations guests have described having with apparitions, some of these seem more like intelligent activity. It is always possible that both are taking place, but the source of energy that the spirits are using can be coming from underground water. Although St. Augustine is surrounded by a river, this location is more towards the center of town. It would be interesting to see if there is an underground spring system or flowing water that could be a source for the spirit's energy.

You also have to consider that being a hotel and a public building can add to the energy as well. We have mentioned this in other chapters, but buildings that have high traffic tend to have heightened reports of paranormal activity. The theory related to this is that all of the different living souls that pass through a concentrated area can affect spiritual energy both positively or negatively. This building is a hotel and was once a public courthouse. Most people believe that spirits can feed on fear and hatred in order to draw on that negative energy and use it to manifest. In our research we have found that the opposite can also take place. We believe that spirits can also draw on positive energy as well and having thousands of people entering and exiting a location can add to that energy.

As for the reports from employees and patrons about the sounds of children running, laughing, and playing, we heard a possible explanation for this from two other locations that we have visited that were hotels back around the same time period. During those days, those who had the means to stay at these lavish locations, would sometimes travel with their entire families. In the evenings, after dinner, the children were dismissed to go to special areas with their nannies. The parents then spent the rest of the night socializing with their friends, not worrying about their children or what they were up to since the nannies would be babysitting them. These special areas were to be supervised by nannies from the various families, but it was also a time for those women to socialize with each other, get caught up on the latest gossip, or share stories about their bosses. Large groups of children would spend the nights together, running around playing, laughing, and sometimes getting into mischief since they were not always so well supervised. This could explain why these locations have these reports of this type of residual activity.

Our Experiences and Opinions

We did not have the opportunity to go inside of the Casa Monica Hotel, but we were by the building several times. We went by the location the first time during our buggy ride and then again on our ghost walk, and we heard the ghost stories from both tour guides. We find it extremely amusing that the hotel management does not admit to any paranormal activity since one of the previous owners, Henry Flagler, believed in spiritualism and the paranormal. Nearly every other building in the area has haunted tours and welcome guests who are seeking the supernatural, but the owners of this location are based out of Orlando. I think we need to go back to this location wearing paranormal shirts and just ask those at the counter if they would mind us walking around and looking at the lobby, maybe even carrying a recorder with us. Either that or stay in room 511 or 411 one night. Marianne's vote is to stay in room 411.

16 FLAGLER COLLEGE

PANICd#: 1525

74 King St
St. Augustine, FL 32084

A Little History

For the wealthy living on the East coast of the country in the mid-1800s, a popular destination during the long, dreary, and harsh winter months was Florida. The area surrounding St. Augustine was avoided, however, since there were no lavish hotels to support the needs of those with the means to make the journey down to the city. A man named, Henry M. Flagler (who was the co-founder of the Standard Oil Company), saw this need when he traveled down to the area from Jacksonville, Florida while on honeymoon with his second wife. As he pondered about the situation less than luxurious St. Augustine (and areas farther South), he decided to embark on one of his largest projects since his assistance with the formation of Standard Oil. He decided to build a rail service that ran South through Florida, and of course, the construction of the grand and luxurious, Ponce de Leon Hotel.

The Ponce de Leon was to have many new features and be the first in many different construction tasks. It was the first building to be built from poured concrete, taking advantage of the local coquina stone as aggregate. The building was also wired for electricity during construction, with power being supplied by direct current generators supplied by Flagler's good friend, Thomas Edison. As an aside, electricity was so new when the power was first turned on in the building, Flagler had to hire staff to turn on and off light switches since the guests were too afraid to do it themselves. (There were 4100 lights which needed turned on and off for the guests whenever they wanted.)

The interior of the building was to be as luxurious as possible. Flagler commissioned Louis Comfort Tiffany to assist with the design elements of the interior including all of the stained glass and chandeliers. He also hired well known artists and furniture designers of the time to in order to ensure that the Ponce de Leon was the "crown jewel" of not only St. Augustine, but the entire state of Florida. Just some of these artist were George W. Maynard, who painted the murals in the rotunda and dining room and noted Italian artist Virgilio Tojetti who painted the ceiling murals in the Grand Parlor. As a side note, George W. Maynard went on a decade later and painted the murals in the Treasurers Gallery at the Thomas Jefferson building of the Library of Congress.

The building sits on 5 acres of land that was once a salt marsh. Construction began in 1885 and was completed in 1887. The design was in the Spanish Renaissance style by architects John Carrere and Thomas Hastings and was built by James McGuire and Joseph McDonald. It was massive with 540 rooms, a 10,000 foot courtyard with an amazing fountain with 12 frogs that make a giant sundial, a huge dining hall that could seat 700, private parlors, steam heat, and as mentioned before, electricity. What it did not have though, private bathrooms. The only private bathroom was in Flagler's private suite – this almost immediately was altered as private bathrooms just seemed necessary.

The twin towers have quite an interesting design and past. They were originally designed to be water storage tanks which contained 8,000 gallons of water each. This was sufficient enough water for the guests of the hotel during the hot and dry summer months.

The opening was held January 10, 1888. Among the guests that very first night- Ulysses S. Grant, Rockefeller, and Vanderbilt.

During World War II, the hotel was utilized by the U.S. Coast Guard as a training center, and they converted one of the towers into a brig. From 1942-1945, thousands of young recruits received their advanced training at the Ponce de Leon, and it is very likely that the brig had some use. After the war, the facility once again was returned to a hotel.

In April of 1967, the doors of the Ponce de Leon closed for good with a final grand dinner party and dance; held in the dining hall. It did not sit vacant for too long though as in 1968, Dr. F. Roy Carlson, the President of Mount Ida Junior College in Newton Massachusetts (and his organization), purchased the hotel for $1.5 million dollars in hopes of converting it into the Flagler Junior College. Many renovations and retrofits had to be performed for the conversion form a luxurious hotel into a college and they spent another $21 million dollars on these projects. The college eventually began to have financial issues. In 1971, the Henry Flagler's grandson, Lawrence Lewis, stepped in and became a driving force to not only reopen the college, but to expand it from a small Junior college to a four-year, liberal arts college. Lewis raised millions and even contributed some of his personal money to help finish off the renovations and restore the buildings to serve as the beautiful Flagler College.

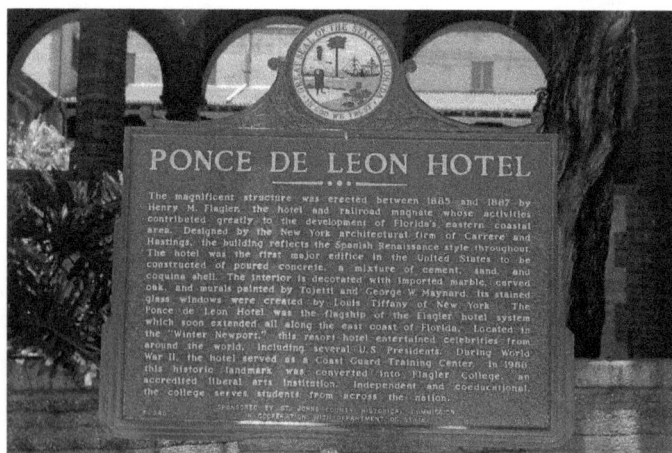

Ghostly Encounters, Stories, and/or Folklore

Henry Flagler was a peculiar and particular man who had his own set of beliefs that he followed religiously. He insisted that every room in the hotel be different in some way. This not only inflated his budget, but it also put a great burden on his contractors, designers, and decorators. Flagler didn't care about any of that, he wanted what he wanted.

There is story that relates to the special tile on the floor in the main hallway. When the tillers were working on the floor, Mr. Flagler stopped by to check out the building progress. Someone mentioned that the floor was "perfect." In response to the comment, Flagler took his toe and moved one of the tiles saying, "only God is perfect." That tile still remains out of place today and is pointed out in the.

There is more story about this tile piece too. Flagler requested that on his death, every window and door of the hotel would be opened so that his spirit would be able to leave and go into the afterlife which is a very common Victorian tradition. While his funeral was being conducted, a janitor went around and closed all of the windows and doors. A gust of wind reportedly entered the auditorium moved and toward the windows, as if it was the spirit of Flagler trying to beat the janitor to get out of one of the last remaining open windows. The story goes that as the wind reached the final open window, the janitor closed it and accidentally trapped Flagler's spirit in the building. Legend also states that the wind then bounced off the closed window and landed on the tile piece that we mentioned above. Some say if you look closely, you can see a picture of Henry Flagler's face in that tile.

In the late 1960's, not long after the opening of the college, a student heard the story about the tile. Late one night, he went down to the main hallway where the tile is located and invited Mr. Flagler up to his room for a visit. Some say that Flagler has been haunting the dorm area ever since.

There is a story about Flagler's second wife, Ida Alice Flagler. Ida was not the most mentally stable individual. Some say she went crazy over the many affairs that Henry had and eventually she ended up dying in a sanatorium of tuberculosis. (It probably did not help the Flagler kept a room for his mistress right in the hotel…) There are those who say she can be seen floating around the college looking at the various art pieces. She has also be seen facing a wall and beating on it, silently screaming. She is quite often seen staring at a place on the wall where a large painting of Flagler once stood.

Another story is about an apparition of a woman dressed in blue. The story is that she was the mistress of one of the guests and was pregnant. The guest was supposed to leave his wife and run away with the woman, but he kept delaying this. One night when they were leaving, the woman tripped over her blue dress and fell down the steps to her death. There are several who report seeing her apparition around or within the dorm rooms, as if she is waiting for her lover to leave with her.

Another story boasts and apparition of a little boy. One story claims that he died in the hotel due to a disease in the early part of the 20th century. Another is that he was a relative of a college student and he fell to his death from a balcony. The apparition of the little boy has been seen from time to time and likes to play pranks on the living by moving their personal items or turning on lights and water.

Other apparitions and shadow figures have been see as well. Some have reported seeing the apparition of a woman hanging from the chandler in the fourth floor "mirror room". This woman is reported to be a mistress of Flagler. He apparently locked her in this room when his wife surprisingly showed up at the hotel in order to avoid the two women running together. The mirror room was built to be a psychomanteum, which is a room designed to alter one's mood and contact the dead. Séances used to be held in this room by wealthy guests and it was too much for the mistress. She started to go mad staring at herself in the mirrors and eventually hung herself from the chandelier.

Students who stay in the dorms report paranormal activity late in the evenings and early mornings. One report is that between midnight and 1 am you will hear the sound of an old typewriter and smell cigar smoke. Now one may think this is a naughty student up late writing a paper, but how many students use typewriters today? Is it perhaps instead a ghost student from long ago? Or could it be one of the authors who stayed there when the building was the Ponce de Leon Hotel - Mark Twain, Ernest Hemmingway, or Robert Frost? Another repost is of a figure dressed in black who stands and watches them sleep.

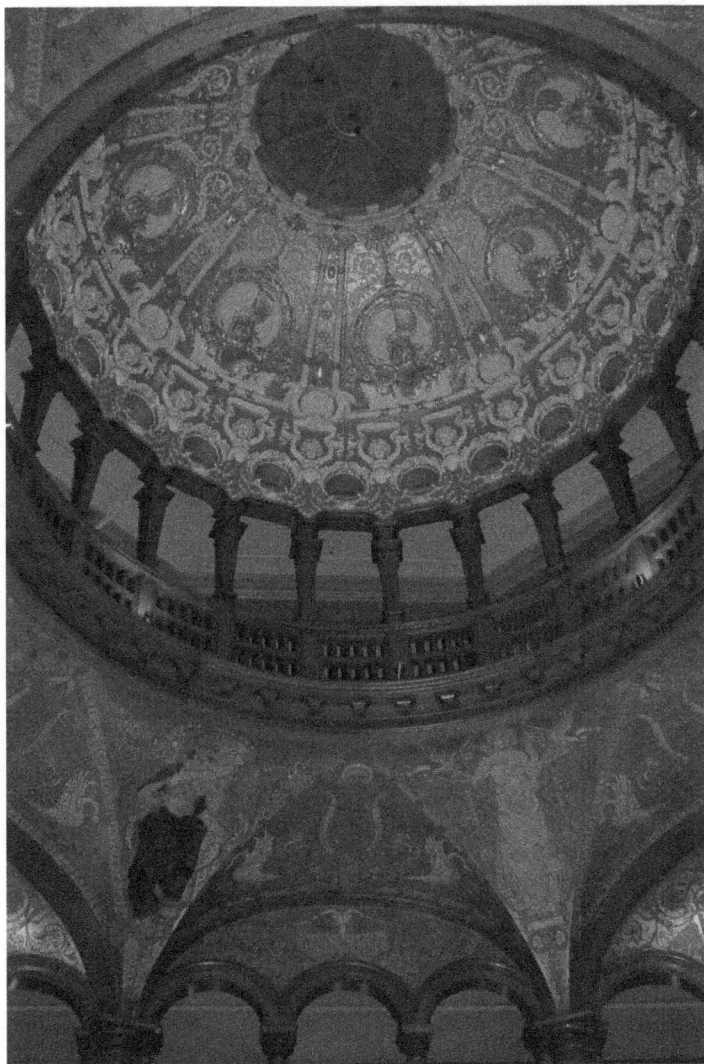

Paranormal Claims

- The apparition of a woman has been seen hanging from the chandler in the fourth floor mirror room.
- Reports of screams coming from the mirror room.
- Many claim to see the face of Henry Flagler peering back at them from one of the tiles on the floor.
- The apparition of Henry Flagler has been reported throughout all of the buildings on campus. (As if he was still around keeping an eye on things.)
- Many claim to see the apparition of a pregnant women dressed in blue. Thought to be a woman who tripped over her blue dress when she was leaving the hotel and fell down the steps to her death.
- A student reported hearing a typewriter late at night as if an author was working on a very important manuscript. It would type constantly until the wee hours of the morning. This may not sound strange for a college, but she reported that the typewriter sounded like an old vintage model with a bell that signaled you to manually hit the carriage return.
- A student reported that sometimes when she was in the shower, she would hear what sounded like a worker come in, sit down his tool box, kneel down on the floor, and whistle as tune as if he was going to work. When she looked out of the shower, there was nobody there.
- Reports of figures in black watching students sleep.

Potential of Haunting

With this building previously being a hotel, you have all of those high levels of positive and negative energy associated with it. Great experiences of happiness or great sadness will be experienced behind closed doors and that type of energy can become trapped or leave an impression on the environment within the walls of the building. This is not even to mention all of the famous individuals who stayed there and shared great conversations and time with their esteemed colleagues.

There was an actual room built in the hotel to host and conduct séances. Séances in any form are an activity that is known to open up and invite spirits into this realm. Without proper closure, those spirits can become trapped here not allowing them the opportunity to return back to their dimension if the activity is not closed out properly. Similar to using a Ouija board, if you open a doorway or invite the spirits in, you need to close that door way and allow the spirits to leave.

Since the opening of the hotel until the present day, hundreds of thousands of people have entered the doors of the hotel and college. There is a theory that states that when you have high traffic in one area, there can be energy that is left behind. Also, all of these people can become a source of energy for the spirits to draw upon that can be used to help the spirits manifest. This is also seen in areas such as train stations and airports.

Although the building was built from poured concrete, the aggregate of that concrete was the local coquina. As we have mentioned many times already, coquina contains limestone, which is a known element to house and retain paranormal energy. Like several other buildings in St. Augustine, the entire building is made of that element.

This is a photograph of the infamous tile that is making the design imperfect.

Our Experiences and Opinions

We visited Flagler College during the day and took the day tour. One of the campus jobs for the students is to conduct the tours after learning the history of Henry Flagler and the building. Of course, we took this tour before we had any clue about the paranormal or even the activity that was reported in the building. When we go back, we will be loaded up and ready to make some audio recordings and shoot more photos.

On a personal, non-paranormal note though, they have one of the original chairs from the Ponce de Leon Hotel and on the tour they let you sit in it if you want. I, Marianne, was super excited to sit in it. Just thinking that one of our Presidents, Rockefeller, Vanderbilt, Mark Twain, or Robert Frost etc. could have sat in the same chair made me overflow with excitement.

Finally, we were quite shocked when the tour guide explained that you could not just buy lodging for one night when Flagler first opened the hotel. In fact, you had to agree that your stay would be quite lengthy. I have wracked my brain, but I do not remember the exact length your stay had to be… it was ether a month or the entire season. I just remember being totally shocked that that was the minimum stay.

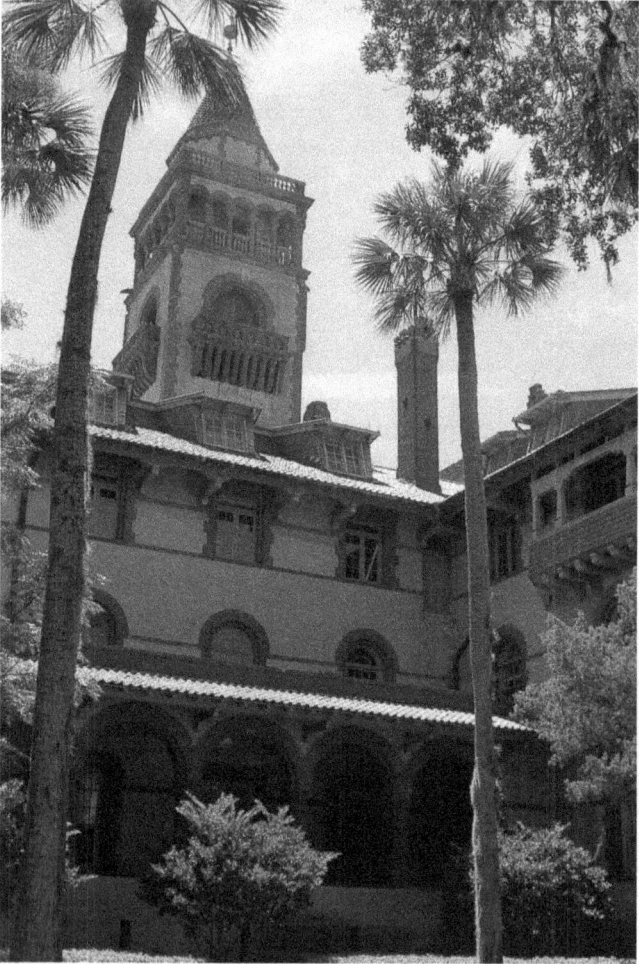

17 THE CASABLANCA INN

PANICd#: 1524

24 Avenida Menendez
St. Augustine, FL 32084

A Little History

Built in 1914, this Mediterranean revival style two story home with a carriage house soon became a boarding house for travelers visiting St. Augustine. For most of the building's history it has been a boarding house or an inn. In the early years, it was called the Mantanzas Hotel. When ownership changed around 1920, the widow who purchased the property changed the name to the Bayfront

Boarding House. After a few years, she again renamed her establishment the Casablanca Inn.

During the 1920s and 1930s, the widow who owned the Inn took great pride in running a clean, comfortable boarding house, offering excellent meals, and making the Casablanca a popular place to for travelers due to the warm hospitality she provided. The inn became so popular that guests would have to call in advance to make reservations.

Most of the guests staying at the inn were either traveling salesmen and G-Men who would be in the area looking for illegal alcohol. This was the time of prohibition and the bay outside of St. Augustine was a well-known stop for rum-runners from Cuba and Puerto Rico who were smuggling rum into the country. G-Men would come to the area and would wait for the rum-runners to unload their cargo and arrest those who picked up the illegal rum to bring it up north. They would sometimes just smash the bottles and barrels right there in the bay.

Ghostly Encounters, Stories, and/or Folklore

Sometime in the 1920s, the widow ran into some financial issues and was in jeopardy of losing the inn that she came to love. She either came up with the idea or someone approached here with an idea to make some extra income by assisting the bootleggers.

Now almost all of her guests, including the G-Men, would like a little nightcap before they went to bed. Since alcohol was illegal, she could kill two birds with one stone if she helped the bootleggers. She would get a little something for her help from them and get some alcohol for her guests -- discreetly. She knew most of the federal agents and she knew when they were in town since they would stay at the Casablanca. All she would have to do is signal the rum-runners when the agents were not in town and they would come into the bay to drop off their illegal liquor. The way she signaled them was she would go up to the top of her building to the widows walk and stand there swinging a lantern late at night. If the agents were in town, there would be no signal on the building and everyone knew not to come near the town and they would just drop anchor off the coast awaiting her single that all was clear. For this service, she was compensated quite handsomely. She would even allow the bootleggers to stay at the inn by payment of rum and liquor so she would have what her guest wanted in the secrecy of the night. With this extra little side job, she was able to take care of her guests and keep her Inn.

At one point, she was questioned by the G-Men, but was deemed not a suspect. She wasn't arrested by agents and lived very well for the rest of her life as she made a fortune. She died and was buried in Huguenot Cemetery.

A slightly different story tells the tale of a bit of a tragedy. It claims that the lady was a young widow who came up with the plan, but that she waved the lantern when there were G-men in town. She wound up falling in love with one of the smugglers and her heart was broken when she learned that the one she loved was killed during a big storm at sea after she had waved the lantern to warn him not to come into town.

There are some who have reported seeing a wispy, fog-like apparition appear in various locations on the inside and outside of the building and a light that appears on the catwalk. There are reports of someone stepping on the floorboards, people talking, and the sounds of children playing as well.

We found a report on Trip Advisor for this location from a couple who spent four nights at this location and were not aware that there was any paranormal activity associated with the location. For the record, we have found it amazingly impossible to find any older hotel or inn that does not have reports of paranormal activity. However, the comments that they posted were quite interesting.

One of the reports that they provided was that in their room there was a light that would turn on and off by itself. Thinking that this could be a short in the lamp, the husband unplugged it, yet it continued to go on and off by itself. The entire time that they were there, they had the sense there was someone else in the room and the woman would not take a shower or bath since she had the feeling that someone or something was watching her. After their stay, they reported of being very sleep deprived since they also had to muffle their ears with their pillows to deaden the sounds of footsteps and knocks in the room during the night.

There are many reports on Trip Advisor that are excellent reviews for this location, so we are not trying to say that this is not an excellent inn. Just be aware that it is haunted.

Paranormal Claims

- Various people from several locations have reported seeing what appears to be a person waving a lantern from the widow's walk at the inn, although there is nobody up there.
- Staff and guests have heard the sound of footsteps on the inn's floorboards.
- Staff and guests have heard the sound of people talking in rooms where there is no one staying.
- Items are moved and found in odd places or sometimes borrowed, but are always returned.
- Sometimes the scent of oranges, that is associated with the woman, can permeate the room for an instant.
- It has been said that a lady's unseen presence has been felt by some folks and some people have thought to have experienced her gentle touch.
- Children have been heard playing around the inn when there are none around.

Potential of Haunting

The only thing separating this location and the bay of

the Matanzas River is a small two lane road in front of the building. That large body of moving water is a great energy source for spirits who may be lingering in the Casablanca Inn or it could be a source of energy for residual activity. This location has always been some kind of boarding house or hotel with several guests. The only long term residents would be the original owner or innkeepers. We have mentioned this in many other chapters and this building would be considered to be a high traffic area.

Another thing to consider is the fear factor that may have transpired here during the time when the illegal activity took place. That energy could have also been transferred into the environment each night when the woman would get on top of the building to signal the rum-runners. She had to have several nights where she feared being caught and emotions would have been high.

Our Experiences and Opinions

We heard about the paranormal claims of the inn during our ghost walk and we actually started our buggy ride in front of this building. We did not investigate here, but just looking at the place you get a sense that there is a presence or something there looking back at you. Even as you leave the area, it is as if someone is watching you to see what you are going to do. We have highly considered trying to get a room here when we return to St. Augustine in the future, not just for the paranormal claims at this building, but for the location of the building as well. This location is well within walking distance of almost all of the buildings and locations within the historical district of St. Augustine and the view of the bay is wonderful from here.

18 THE OLDEST WOODEN SCHOOLHOUSE

PANICd#: 1895

14 St George St
St. Augustine, FL 32084

A Little History

The Oldest Wooden Schoolhouse is located near the Old City Gates. According to multiple sources, this building was built around 200 years ago. Tax records show that the building was present in 1716 though making at least 300 years old. This is one of the earliest original buildings remaining from that was built when the town of St. Augustine was established. Many students attended this little school over the years beginning in 1788 and is theschoolhouse was also the first co-ed school since it educated both girls and boys together beginning in that same year. The last graduating class was the class of 1864.

In approximately 1780 Juan Genoply, the original schoolmaster, purchased the property. It was a single level at the time. It was made from bald cypress and red cedar. The building consisted of just one room, but there were also a separate kitchen, outhouse (privy), and well for drinking water. When he married and started to have a family, he needed a place for his family so an addition of a second story was added for him and his family to live in. To this day, the building has no electricity or running water.

Most people immediately notice the large chain and anchor that is on the building. The chain wraps around the entire building and was added in 1937 when a hurricane threatened St. Augustine. The chain was an attempt to secure the historical building so it would not be lost. Apparently it worked as the building still stands today.

After the addition of the second floor, the first floor was used for the classroom and the schoolmaster and his wife would live upstairs above the small classroom on the newly constructed second floor. The kitchen always remained separate from the main building, which is believed to be the reason the wooden building survived with no fire issues through the years. They also did this so that it would not create excessive heat in the building during the summer months of Florida.

The location has several of the cooking utensils that they used in those days on display for the visitors to see how it used to be when the school was active. Also on display are artifacts and copies of books the pupils used to use for studying.

Juan Genopoly was known to have three wives who died while living in the house.

Ghostly Encounters, Stories, and/or Folklore

We never heard of any ghost stories about this building when we were in town and took the ghost tours, but if you visit the location in person, you can tell that there is something going on there. Especially with the creepy animatronic characters they have showing the daily routines of the school back in the 1700's and early 1800's. We did find something while researching this book though.

It turns out that the school house is most likely being haunted by a young woman who lost her daughter in the early 1800s. There have been sightings of the woman who is dressed in period clothing, her dark hair pulled into a bun, and she is looking out the second-floor window. A psychic once made contact with the spirit and reported that the women is still mourning because her daughter died when she was away. People who have walked by the building report seeing the women at the second-floor window, looking west as if she is waiting for someone to return home.

This story is not part of the local's ghost stories. However, we would like to ask about it in more detail and interview some of the tour guides when we return. They now have a paranormal investigation at the is location, so perhaps we will hear more about this next time we visit.

As far as other stories and folklore, we did find information about a class reunion of the final graduating class from the schoolhouse. They met in 1931 and told stories of their experiences including being punished by being put into a small closet under the stairs and that they had no desks, they usually just sat on the coquina floor with their books in their laps. Their reunion was recorded by the Eastman Kodak Co.

Paranormal Claims

- The apparition of a woman dressed in period clothing has been seen looking out the second floor window.
- Strange sounds and noises have been heard and recorded.

Potential of Haunting

This building has been in St. Augustine since the town was established well over 200 - 300 years ago. It has seen hundreds of thousands of people come and go throughout the years both when it was a school and as a tourist attraction. Being a school also provides for the potential of paranormal activity. School buildings house staff and students who experience heightened emotions on occasion and over many years this energy can transfer into the environment. This energy can become trapped and can be fuel used for residual activity. Marianne can attest to the fact that a teacher's classroom is like a second home. In fact, most teachers spend more of their time in their classroom than they do in their actual homes. It is a theory that entities return to places they loved...will Marianne return to her classroom in her afterlife? Did schoolmaster Genoply return to his?

It is also reported that there were three known deaths in the little dwelling; the wives of the former schoolmaster. It is possible that one of these spirits is still there and is the one that is being reported looking out the top window on occasion. Sometimes when the living pass on, they do not realize that they have and the spirit can become trapped on earth until a new doorway is opened for them so that they can cross over into the other realm. This could be the case here as we have seen and read many reports like this across the country.

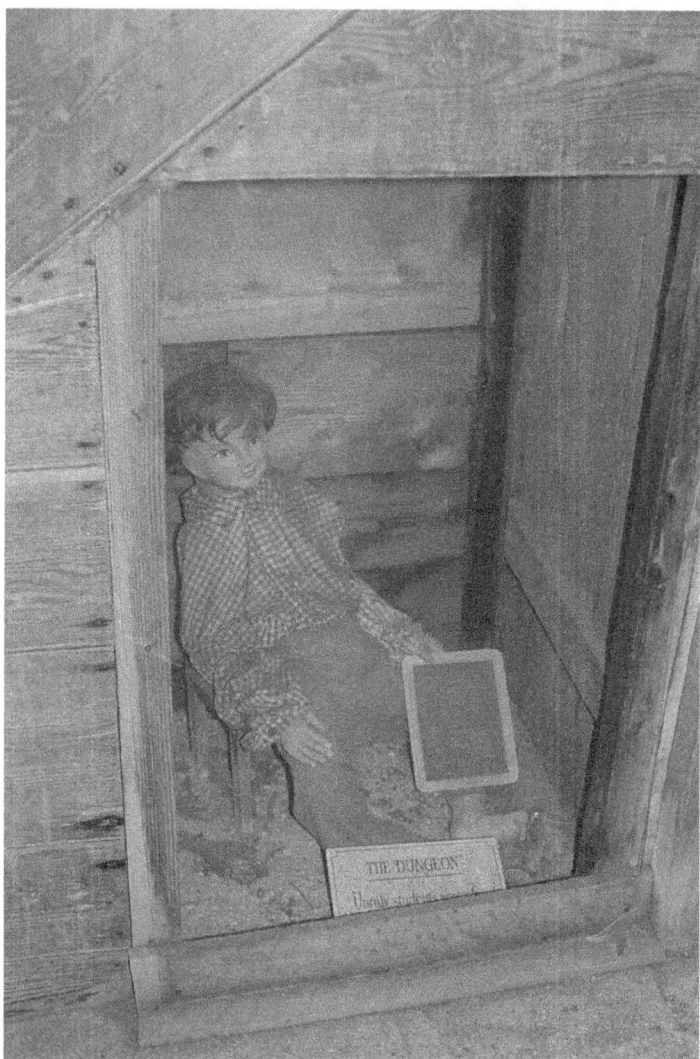

Our Experiences and Opinions

There are several "oldest" or "first" type buildings in St. Augustine. It makes sense since St. Augustine was the first city established in America. As a tourist, you try to visit as many of these locations as you possibly can, but I can tell you, this place does have a creep factor that looms around the building and definitely inside with the animatronic characters. We actually visited this building in 2006, but as we were looking through some of the pictures we took there, I remembered right away that I had been uneasy and worried that we were going to be attacked by the children who all looked like Chucky dolls in period clothing. We didn't have any anomalies on our photographs though, which is what we were trying to find. I guess this location is back on the list to visit in the future. We will even try to do a full paranormal investigation at this location since this now is an option.

19 OUR THEORIES ON WHY ST. AUGUSTINE IS SO HAUNTED

As we look back on the time we have spent in St. Augustine, we reflect and try to form our theories as to why this little town has had so many reported paranormal claims. Let's review some of the personal and geographical history of the location to help us understand why this city is a hotbed for ghost sightings and other paranormal activity.

First, let's look at territory occupation. This town has been occupied by Native Americans, Spaniards, the British, and Americans. Almost every time it changed hands, there was a battle. Civilians were uprooted from their homes and either died or were forced to spend time within the walls of Castillo de San Marcos for protection purposes. That is a great deal of bad energy that has accumulated over time in a very small area.

Second, the foundation of the town itself can explain some of the occurrences. Almost all of the buildings, including the large fort Castillo de San Marcos and the streets themselves, are made of the local quarried coquina stones. The beaches on the coast of St. Augustine were found to be abundant with this hard stone. The builders of the town would cut out these stones and bring them into the village to build the town. So, what is coquina stone? It is a combination of highly compressed mollusk shells and limestone. A highly proposed and accepted theory in paranormal investigations is that limestone can be a great storage for residual energy and ghostly sightings. The entire town of St. Augustine was built with this stone.

Third, St. Augustine is a beautiful location. When you have a place that is as beautiful as St. Augustine, it is going to attract a large number of visitors each year. The town's population is around 13,500, but in 2011, the state of Florida estimated that there were about 85 million visitors to Florida. With St. Augustine being towards the border of Florida if you are coming down the east coast, it is easy to believe that a large number of these visitors have either stopped or passed through this beautiful town. This is a high number of bodies in a small area leaving behind all different forms of energy. There is a paranormal theory that highly traffic areas such as train stations, theaters, hotels, hospitals, etc. can stir up paranormal activity from all of the energy that passes through these locations. We believe that this can be the same for a larger geographical area as well, just like the entire town of St. Augustine.

Fourth, would be the geographical location. If you look at St. Augustine on a map, you will notice it is surrounded by water on three sides. Although the town sits a little bit inland from the Atlantic Ocean, the Matanzas River runs on the south, east, and west sides of the town. Another paranormal theory suggests that water can be a catalyst for stirring up paranormal activity as moving water releases a great deal of energy that then becomes available for entities to use.

There are probably several more theories that can be developed, but just these four alone (battles and war, limestone, high tourist activity, and water) with the added fact that St. Augustine is the oldest city in the country, and has immense amounts of history, it is a wonder that you just don't see apparitions walking around on the streets all day every day like some scene from the movies. For those of us into paranormal investigations and research, we know it does not work that way and you never know when the spirits would like to communicate. We just leave you with this, if you go to St. Augustine for a visit, just keep your eyes open, your recorders running, and take a ton of pictures. You never know what you might capture.

20 WHAT EQUIPMENT TO USE WHILE TRAVELING

There are many different pieces of equipment that you can use during paranormal investigations and we are not going to take up space in this book to go over all of them. What we are going to do is provide of list of basic equipment you can use, especially if you are flying and need to go through TSA. I have had many occasions where I had to take out a device, explain it was for ghost hunting, and turn it on for TSA since they never heard of the item before. If this happens to you, just comply and do as they ask. There is no need to be tied up for questioning over a ghost hunting device.

The following is a checklist of items in priority order. Depending on where you are going, these devices can even be disguised as other touristy devices or pieces of equipment, especially if you run into a location that does not want to admit that there are paranormal claims.

DEFINITELY NEEDED

____ Digital Camera: There is no specific type or brand of camera that is actually needed and a lot of people will use their cell phone. We prefer to use a camera that can recharge the flash rather quickly since we take 3-4 photos at the same thing from the same angle. We may capture 200-300 photos from any given location. With it being digital, snap away. You never know what you might capture.

____ Digital Recorder: I learned from a great friend of mine, Mike Mizenko, to always have your digital recorder running. You never know what you will capture or when you will capture it. We have recorded some of our best evidence when we least expected it, so make sure you have a digital recorder on you that has fresh batteries. You can also use your recorder to take notes thus eliminating the need for a notebook and pen or pencil. If you experience something physical such as a cold spot or an energy burst, just tag it on your recorder.

____ Mini Flashlight: Most ghost tours are at night; in the dark. Most buildings that you investigate will have the lights turned out. Having a little light to help with stairs or to inspect objects is nice. Just be sure abide by any light restrictions given by ghost tour guides and try not to bother anyone else on any tours you are on.

OPTIONAL

____ KII EMF Meter: Since these are small devices, you can also have one of these with you as well. The only thing is, it can get a little bulky if you want to record the KII results with video. Our digital camera also does video and can double as a video camera, but if you have a camera, separate video camera, a digital recorder, and a KII meter walking around, people are surely going to ask what you are doing. We sometimes take KII meters with us on ghost walks or tours, but lately the ones we have been on have them already and let you use theirs. If they have them, don't crack out your own to be impressive. They will try to get all of their materials back at the end of the tour and will assume that you are holding their KII meter after the tour and not your own. They may not believe it is yours until they count their devices.

____ OVILUS: We like to use the OVILUS at night in our room when we stay at a haunted bed and breakfast or when walking through cemeteries. It works well in rooms at bed and breakfasts as it is not loud and obnoxious to fellow guests and we always visit cemeteries on trips and we like to see if we pick up any responses near headstones. I did take mine on the airplane in my carry-on and had to explain to the TSA what it was. They asked me to turn it on when going through security, but that was about it. The OVILUS works great when you have a digital recorder going too. It records the OVILUS responses for posterity.

WHAT WE PROBABLY WOULD NEVER TAKE

____ MEL METER: Although we use this pretty heavily during investigations, I don't think I would travel with my Mel Meter. One of the goals when traveling is to travel lightly and you can be alright without this device if you have to leave it behind.

____ DVR SYSTEM: Unless you have a place booked and scheduled for a full private investigation, this is just common sense. How could you walk into the lobby of a haunted hotel and ask them if you can run cables and set up a DVR System?

____ SB7 / SB11: Again, just common sense. These devices emit too much noise that would draw way to much attention to yourself.

____ INFRARED THERMOMETER GUN: Absolutely not. What do you think this would look like when your checked luggage and/or carry-on is being x-rayed? You will definitely lose some time with TSA with this little gadget.

There is no reason why you cannot take a simple, normal vacation and add a little bit of ghost hunting to it. We have been doing this since 2010 and are always looking for a ghost tour or a ghost walk when we are in new locations. If we cannot find a tour, then we look up historical locations that are in the area and try to do some paranormal research on our own. Either way, have a couple small, inconspicuous devices on hand and take basic tours. You can turn them into small personal ghost hunts. You will never know what you can capture until you try.

TIP: Always have an audio recorder recording. You never know what you will pick up on your recordings, and this will help serve as documentation later when you try to recall the history about the location.

21 TIPS FOR INVESTIGATING WHILE TRAVELING

The following are a few tips you can use to perform some investigations while you are traveling. Even if you take the family out for a vacation at the beach or spend some time with family members across the country, you can always find some ways to perform paranormal investigations.

- **Research, research, and then research.** Prior to traveling to the area of your vacation, perform a little research to find locations that may have some potential hauntings. See Tips to Finding Locations With Paranormal Activity.

- **Be the tourist.** There is no reason why you cannot be the stereotypical tourist when it comes to visiting paranormal locations while traveling. Try to document and record everything you can. Who knows when you will have a chance to return in the future? One of the things that has helped us when putting together this book, is that Marianne makes sure to take photos of placards that describe areas or buildings. This way, when you are going back over your photos, you can remember what you were looking at in the first place. Let's face it we all forget things. There is nothing wrong with using a little photographic evidence to help refresh your memory.

- **Don't pack your batteries.** Why have extra weight in your luggage? Find a local store and purchase your batteries there. This is just a tip we have implemented over the past few years and it will cut down some weight in your luggage.

- **Clear off your memory cards**. Nothing is worse than to be trapped out on a vacation with no laptop and your digital recorder or camera SD card is full. You can buy new cards, but it is just as easy to take some time and clear them off before you leave. This way, everything that you collect while on vacation is information related to that vacation. (Although Marianne did have a paranormal experience in Gettysburg while standing at a paranormal location deleting old photos from a camera – don't worry, they had been copied over previously and just not deleted. Cliffhanger until the Gettysburg volume of Our Haunted Travels!)

- **Plan ahead.** Plan your vacation time and dinners based on ghost walks or tours. Most of these are scheduled and conducted during the weekend. Sometimes you may find tours that are going on every night; however, a good rule of thumb is that they generally only on Thursday through Sunday nights. If you want to go on one of these tours, try to get your tickets online and book them in advance. You will want to try to get to the locations early too so you can get a good spot on the tour that is close to the tour guide. See Tips for Ghost Tours and Walks.

- **Go to where things happened.** If you know the history and paranormal claims for a location, try to go into the buildings where there are claims-- most historical locations will have tours. Find the areas where the history or the claims took place. This is where you want to get pictures and ask the spirits questions. If nothing else, you can support or debunk claims.

- **Always have your recorder running.** Whenever you enter the grounds of a location, start recording on your recorder. You never know what you will capture and when you will capture it. We have our recorders running constantly. Sometimes I have mine in a shirt pocket and Marianne has hers in an outer pocket of her purse. If you are recording outdoors, try to develop a way to muffle the wind. We lost a few recordings that we know we heard something coming through, but the wind noise was just too much. Lesson learned.

- **Ask questions.** If you see employees or if there is a tour guide, don't be afraid to ask questions. Most of the time these people welcome interaction with visitors and you will be amazed as to what information you can uncover that has not been documented.

- **Find areas with low traffic.** If you cannot find an area within a building to perform an EVP session, consider corridors and elevators. You will probably not find the living in these locations, but it is possible to capture some spirits. If you are in a spot where there are no people around, this will help cut down on some evidence contamination.

- **Keep your sessions short.** This is something we are constantly trying to work on. Having hours of recordings to listen to can be daunting at times. Quick sessions can be easily reviewed and can sometimes yield surprising results. With us running our recorders constantly, we always stop them and start them up again if we are doing an EVP session. This helps out tremendously when reviewing evidence.

- **Snap, snap, snap photos**. Take lots and lots of pictures. Try taking multiple photos with the same perspective (or point of view), especially in areas where there are paranormal claims. You never know what you will collect. If the location does not care that you take photos, then take as many as you can. Marianne will get details of architecture, art, or items within a location and in the future when you are going back over your evidence, you will find these photographs to be a treasure. Look at the photos we have in this book. These were take over seven years ago (at the time of this writing), and I am glad that she is so thorough as they have helped refresh my memory. They show you not only the location, but objects, locations of windows and doors, other people on tours etc. that help when reviewing evidence collected.

- **Be cautious.** If the location you are investigating does not want anything to do with paranormal claims or investigations, then don't push it. Try to be inconspicuous while asking questions to the spirits, but this should not stop you from conducting an investigation.

- **Don't get discouraged**. If you don't capture any evidence, don't get discouraged. Just the fact that you tried will build up your confidence for future attempts. To have proof that you were there, where it happened, should be treasure enough. Although we are researching proof of the past, remember to enjoy life with the living as well.

- **If you are asked to leave, leave.** Now, we have not had this happen to us. We are normally pretty quick in and out of locations. If you are asked to leave, common sense would say just leave. Everyone has a bad day and you never know if the people who are working there are having one. It is not worth it to argue with those who are angry, especially if you are on vacation. Though jails are great paranormal hotbeds, I know we only want to visit the inside of jails with previously documented paranormal claims.

- **Look for local paranormal groups.** We sometimes look for local paranormal groups when we are in a new city. A well organized group would be extremely helpful and know all of the hotspots and stories about the area too. Sometimes these groups are the ones that are putting on the ghost tours or walks. We like to seek them out and try to meet with them if we can. We introduce ourselves and tell them what we are doing in the area. These people are glad to share local information, and you can build some long distance friendships as well.

Tip: If you conduct some research in advance, you have more knowledge when asking questions of the tour guides. Spend a little time researching a location before you visit. You will be glad.

22 TIPS FOR FINDING LOCATIONS WITH PARANORMAL ACTIVITY

Whenever we travel to a new city, we always spend some time looking for locations that could have potential activity. Our Haunted Travels have stemmed from this mantra and we hope that these tips will help you on your journey as well.

- **Start with research on the Internet.** Include such words as "paranormal" or "ghosts" in your search. You might be surprised with what comes up. For example: "Dallas Ghosts" turns up about 627,000 Google results. Once you find some of these locations you can start doing a little more in depth research on the location to see what the claims are and plan a stop during your trip. You can also use a website like PANICd.com to find locations within a given area as well.

- **Use mapping software**. Another thing we do is use mapping software to pinpoint how close our hotel is in relation to these locations. Can we walk to them? Do we need to rent a car? Can we take a taxi? Would it be worth the money to go to these locations? Should we consider moving our hotel?

- **Plot an itinerary.** Once we have a list of locations that we would like to visit, we plot them out on a map to determine an itinerary. What order do we want to visit them in? How long is the drive time between locations?

- **What locations to visit.** Some locations that may have more activity than others would be hotels, theaters, old retired jails or prisons, hospitals, or locations that have tragic crimes related to them. Any place that would have high emotional energy could be a location for a potential residual haunting. You can also look for old beautiful homes where the living spent most of their days. There is a theory that spirits may return to the locations that they loved while they were alive.

- **Do the locations offer tours?** You don't have to go on a ghost tour or walk, just going on a regular tour of the location can be good enough. Just remember to have your recorder going and take a lot of pictures.

- **Document the outside of the location.** When you first arrive at the location, try to get pictures of the outside of the building. Also, see if there is signage outside to go with the pictures. If there is a national or state historical registry sign, you will want to get a photo of this as well. Make sure you try to get these when you arrive. We have had a couple of times where tours within the building went into evening hours. It gets dark at night. At a few location we missed the opportunity of getting the photograph or the building or historical markers with the sun out.

- **Ask questions.** If you have decided to take a tour of the location with a tour guide and they are not talking about any of the paranormal information that you may have discovered during your research, there is no reason why you cannot ask them about what you have found or if they have experienced anything. Sometimes it is funny how their voice lowers and they quietly explain their personal ghostly experiences to you. We have had this happen on many different occasions.

- **Ask/Interview locals.** Another way to find locations with paranormal activity is to ask local residents. If you didn't have any luck finding anything at all, ask your servers at the restaurants you visit if they have heard of anything ghostly in town or around the area. Sometimes you can pick up some great tips from locals.

- **Look into the history.** If you are coming up short on locations within the area, look for locations with a strong historical background. We have been to locations that are considered to be some of the most haunted locations in the country and haven't captured anything on the recorder. Now, we have also been to locations rich in history and the spirits would just not stop talking. You will never know when a spirit will want to communicate with you.

- **Local cemeteries tell stories**. If all else fails, look for local cemeteries. I'm not saying that all cemeteries are haunted, but you will find the town's local history in those places and some of them can be the most peaceful and beautiful locations you will ever find. There is nothing wrong with taking some time to pay your respects to those who are interred there. You may even pick up on some names of local historical figures that you may use in your EVP sessions.

Whatever you find or wherever you visit is a checkmark in the win column. We learned the hard way that you have to do a little bit a research to where you are going. You never know what little gems are close to where you will be staying – or even will be in the same room with you.

Tip: Ghost Tours are a great way to gather local history for any town. Most of these tours are either ran by paranormal groups or historical societies. We highly recommend trying to find a ghost tour for any area that you may visit.

23 PARTICIPATING IN GHOST WALKS AND TOURS

Very popular tourist attractions in most cities are ghost walks or ghost tours. Companies have put together tours that you can go on, mostly at night, that explain local folklore and history. Some are put together very well and others are just horrible. We have been on many good ones and we have been on ones that basically provide no local history at all and just tell you what other guests have experienced. How can you tell which ones are good and which ones are bad? Unfortunately, you cannot. The reason is not the tours themselves, but the tour guides.

We suggest, that you just take whatever tours you can find. If they are horrible, you are just out a few dollars. If they are great, you just picked up a little bit more information that you may have not of experienced or ever learned.

Here is a list of a few tips you should consider when participating in ghost walks or tours:

- **Try to book your tours in advance**. If you can purchase your tickets online, this is the way to go. This way, you are guaranteed to have a spot on the tour. Some tours that are in cities heavy with tourists may be booked well in advance. Never think you can just walk up and purchase a ticket. Sometimes you might be lucky, but why take the chance. If you have your tickets in advance, you can plan other activities around your ghost tours too.

- **Record everything you can.** A lot of the tour guides do not like to be video recorded, but they don't have a problem if you have an audio recorder. Others do not like any recordings of any kind. Always ask them before the tour begins if they would mind if you record it. We have captured some EVPs in the past during ghost tours, but it is also kind of cool simply to go back and listen to the tour's audio. You can remember being on the tour again.

- **Take photographs.** Take as many pictures as you possibly can. We have been on a number of tours where the guides encourage you to take photographs. Some of them will also tell you about pictures that other people have taken. We have even been on tours where they have shown us printed photographs from others who have taken the tour. You never know what you might capture.

- **Try to get there early and stay close to the tour guide.** If you running a recorder during the tour, you are going to want to be up towards the front of the tour group. We have noticed that on almost all of the ghost tours we have been on, the tour guides have a tendency to not wait on stragglers when they begin to talk. Maybe they have given the tour several times or maybe they just want to be done for the evening. If you don't keep up with the tour guide, you may miss something important.

- **Try to take your tours as a couple.** If you have someone with a recorder, they can stay towards the front of the group to record the tour guide and the person with the camera can hang towards the back and have more time to take pictures after everyone has filed out of the locations. This is exactly how Marianne and I go on ghost tours.

- **Be prepared to do some walking with good shoes**. We have had tours with stairs, some steep grade walking, and others with long periods of standing in one location listening to the tour guide. Be prepared for being on your feet for several hours. You will probably be entering some locations that are dark as well. Having solid shoes instead of sandals or flip-flops is recommended to avoid stubbed toes.

- **Be prepared to go a couple of hours with no restroom or refreshments.** Most of these tours do not offer breaks and they do not offer any type of refreshments either. If we are on a tour during the summer months, I sometimes get a bottle of water and carry it in one of my pockets. Be prepared to go a long time between breaks during the tours.

- **Do a little research before the tour.** This can sometimes be fun and it can sometimes be curse if you have read or heard contradictory information to what the tour guide is telling you. Although, to read about a location and then have the ability to stand there at the same spot, that feeling just cannot be compared.

- **Pick the middle time for the tour if possible.** When you go to book a tour, see if the tour companies are offering multiple times during the evening. If they are, try to take the time that is in the middle. If you book the one that is early, you may have a lot of children on your tour. Sometimes this can be a distraction to the tour guide and they will also tone down the information presented. If you book the last one very late at night, then you get the teenagers or college kids that like to goof around. They like to pop out of the darkness and scare each other. Which is very distracting to you when you are trying to pay attention to the tour guide. It seems as if the tours in the middle hours are for those who are truly interested. If there are only a couple tours on a given day, then choose the early one. If nothing else, this gives you a little time to go back to a location after the tour to collect some additional evidence without the contamination of a tour group before you call it a night.

- **Take notes.** While you are on the tour, try to take note of where the buildings are located. You may want to visit the locations again during the day to try and collect more information. When the tours are going on at night, you may sometimes lose your bearings and forget how to get back. If you note the address or the names of the buildings in your digital recorder this would be helpful. You might also take notes about what the paranormal claims are for locations. This way you can look into them more at a later time to find more details about events that may lend themselves to the claims made for the location.

We always look for ghost tours when we travel to different places. Even if you are not into ghost stories or the paranormal, you can still enjoy them. You will definitely get a different perspective on the area you are visiting, as well as some great history.

24 TIPS FOR STAYING AT A HAUNTED HOTEL

Whenever we travel, we try to take at least one night and spend it at a haunted location. In most cases these are bed and breakfasts or buildings that have been converted into bed and breakfast hotels. There are also a lot of hotels and motels out there with haunted claims. Most people might not be into this, which is why some of these locations do not like to talk about the spirits who have not checked out, so sometimes it is not easy to find places with paranormal claims. We have also found out that some of the places where we have stayed in the past have had paranormal claims. We just found out way after we checked out. Be sure to do your homework before you travel.

Here are some tips for finding a location where you can spend the night that has paranormal claims and how you can use your room for a little extra paranormal investigating and research:

1. **Research**. Again, research the area looking for bed and breakfast locations with paranormal claims. Once you find one, see if you can find out what rooms or areas that have the most sightings or reported haunted experiences. Sometimes claims can be focused to certain room or hall ways, so make sure to book your room based on the information you can find.

2. **Check to see if the location embraces paranormal claims or if they refuse to admit or promote them.** If the location embraces the claims, when you arrive you have the green light to interview and ask questions. We have had managers at locations pretty much bend over

backwards in getting us access to certain locations and rooms when they knew who we were and what we planned on doing. We have also learned that if the location does not want to admit to the claims, it is just better to leave well enough alone. How can you find this out in advance? First, if they have a section on their website explaining ghost stories or paranormal claims, jackpot. Although, we did have this backfire on one occasion. We actually had a location owner tell us, "No, we just put that on our website to sell some rooms. I don't really believe in that stuff." If it is not on the website, just make an anonymous call and ask them. If you read about the location having paranormal claims on other websites and they don't mention it on theirs, there is no reason why you cannot call and try to corroborate what others say about the location.

3. **Leave a recorder going in your room when you go out for some other adventure.** We always do this. After we check in at a location, get cleaned up, refreshed a little bit, and ready to run out for some other tour or food or whatever, we will start an EVP session and leave the recorder run while we are gone. We tell the spirits that it is there in case they want to make a noise or leave a message. Sometimes we even leave a recorder running all night long while we sleep. Now, we have never done this, but it might be a good idea to leave a video recorder taping while you are gone. You never know what you might capture when the room is "empty".

4. **Ask questions during the tour.** If the location is open minded about the paranormal, ask them questions when they give you a tour of the facility.

Normally a bed and breakfast will show you where all of the different areas are that you need for your stay. However, finding out more about the areas with paranormal claims is more exciting. We showed up early for the tour at a famous bed and breakfast and spent 30-40 minutes with the tour guide alone before others arrived. We gained a wealth of information and made a new friend at the same time. He showed us some photographs that were not normally shown on the tour. You can bet we had our recorders going at that time. These tour guides are there, in most cases, because they love the building and its history and because they want to share information.

5. **Prepare for your night's investigation.** There are a couple of things to keep in mind if you are going to do an investigation in your room late at night before you go to sleep. Keep an eye on what you eat during the day. Nothing can corrupt an EVP session or make it go a different direction than if you have food during the day that might not agree with you. If you plan on investigating that night, make sure you eat a few hours beforehand and have something from the menu that is easy to digest. If you are tired and have to fight to stay awake when you are lying on your bed conducting a session, you have two options. Either you can find a chair to sit in and not lay down during the session or just don't fight being tired. If you had a long day and wish to just sleep, start off your session and just leave your recorder running through the night. You will never know what you will capture.

6. **Be courteous of other guests.** If you only rented a single room in the facility for the night, you want

to be courteous of the other guests that might be staying there as well. This means that you should only conduct your session in your room, unless you have other permission. Also, don't use an SB7/11 or other spirit boxes that make noise. There's no reason to ruin your night or anyone else's.

7. **Secure your equipment if you are going to fall asleep.** It is a good idea to put your recorder someplace that isn't within your bed if you are going to leave it recording during the night. If you are someone who rolls around in their sleep, you could knock it off the bed, roll over on it, muffle the recording, or even just accidently turn it off. Placing it across the room or on a night stand is highly recommend. It would be horrible to wake up and find your digital recorder in pieces on the floor in the morning.

For years, I have avoided staying in locations that had paranormal claims. For me, if I am going to go to my room to relax and sleep, I do not want the spirits bothering me. In recent years, Marianne has changed my opinion on this and we have spent the night at some famous locations within the paranormal world. The first question that we always get in the morning at breakfast, especially if we are wearing one of our paranormal shirts is, "Did you see anything last night?" My response is, "Not really, I was sleeping. We have to listen back to our recordings. How about you? Did you experience anything?" You never know what you will get back as a response. If they are guests or staff who have experienced something, they are dying to tell you. Take this opportunity to join them for breakfast or conduct a quick interview.

BIBLIOGRAPHY

St. Augustine Lighthouse

Donley, Shawn A.. "St. Augustine Lighthouse". Paranormal Activity Network Information Center Database. PANICd.com. www.panicd.com/st-augustine-lighthouse.html. 30 Jan. 2011. Web. 5 Aug. 2017.

"Lighthouse History". St. Augustine Lighthouse. St. Augustine Lighthouse and Maritime Museum. www.staugustinelighthouse.com/history.php. n.d. Web. 30 Jan. 2011.

"Haunted Lighthouses St. Augustine Lighthouse". Zimbo. Lighthouse History. www.zimbio.com/Paranormal/articles/56/Haunted+Ligh thouses+St+Augustine+Lighthouse. n.d. Web. 30 Jan. 2011.

Spanish Military Hospital

Donley, Shawn A.. "Spanish Military Hospital". Paranormal Activity Network Information Center Database. PANICd.com. www.panicd.com/spanish-military-hospital.html. 22 Dec. 2010. Web. 5 Aug. 2017.

"Spanish Colonial Medicine in Saint Augustine Florida". Spanish Military Hospital Museum. Custom A Design. www.spanishmilitaryhospital.com/. n.d. Web. 23 Dec. 2010.

"Spanish Military Hospital Museum in St. Augustine, FL". Vacations Made Easy. VacationsMadeEasy.com . www.vacationsmadeeasy.com/StAugustineFL/pointsOfIn terest/SpanishMilitaryHospitalMuseuminStAugustineFL.cf m. n.d. Web. 23 Dec. 2010.

"The Haunted Spanish Military Hospital Of St. Augustine, Florida". Haunted Places to Go. haunted-places-to-go.com. www.haunted-places-to-go.com/spanish-military-hospital.html. n.d. Web. 5 Aug. 2017.

Tolomato Cemetery

Donley, Shawn A.. "Tolomato Cemetery". Paranormal Activity Network Information Center Database. PANICd.com. www.panicd.com/tolomato-cemetary.html. 23 Dec. 2010. Web. 5 Aug. 2017.

"A Brief History of Tolomato Cemetery". Tolomato Cemetery Preservation Association . tolomatocemetery.com. www.tolomatocemetery.com/History.html. n.d. Web. 31 Dec. 2010.

"Haunted Tolomato Cemetery". The Paranormalistics. Paranormalics.blogspot.com. paranormalistics.blogspot.com/2012/08/haunted-tolomato-cemetery.html. 9 Aug. 2012. Web. 17 May 2015.

"Real Ghost Pictures: The Tolomato Cemetery tragedy - Paranormal 360". Paranormal 360. Paranormal 360. www.paranormal360.co.uk/real-ghost-pictures-the-tolomato-cemetery-tragedy/. 24 Mar. 2015. Web. 17 May 2015.

Old City Gates and Walls, St. Augustine Florida

Cox, Dale. Old City Gates and Walls - St. Augustine, Florida. N.p., n.d. Web. 04 Aug. 2017. http://www.exploresouthernhistory.com/staugustinegate.html

"St Augustine Old City Gates – Kissimmee Paranormal."
Kissimmee Paranormal. N.p., n.d. Web. 04 Aug. 2017.
http://kissimmeeparanormal.com/investigations/st-
augustine-old-city-gates/nggallery/page/1

"Yellow Fever in St. Augustine." VisitStAugustine.com.
N.p., n.d. Web. 04 Aug. 2017.
https://www.visitstaugustine.com/history/old-st-
augustine/yellow-fever.php

Castillo de San Marcos
Donley, Shawn A.. "Castillo de San Marcos". Paranormal
Activity Network Information Center Database.
PANICd.com. www.panicd.com/castillo-de-san-
marcos.html. 17 Jan. 2011. Web. 6 Aug. 2017.

"Castillo de San Marcos". Florida Vaction Travel. florida-
vation-travel.com. florida-vacation-travel.com/castillo-de-
san-marcos.html. n.d. Web. 17 Jan. 2011.

"Castillo de San Marcos - YouTube". Youtube.com.
woofboy111.
www.youtube.com/watch?v=de8OSGVQdsc. 19 Feb.
2007. Web. 17 Jan. 2011.

McWilliams, Alicia. "Ghost Tours St Augustine, Florida -
Castillo De San Marcos". Ezine Articles.
EzineArticles.com. ezinearticles.com/?Ghost-Tours-St-
Augustine,-Florida---Castillo-De-San-
Marcos&id=1625668. 28 Oct. 2008. Web. 17 Jan. 2011.

"Saint Augustine Haunted Fort, Castillo de San Marcos".
HauntedHouses.com. HauntedHouses.com.
www.hauntedhouses.com/states/fl/saint-augustine-
fort.htm. n.d. Web. 9 Aug. 2017.

Aviles Street

Donley, Marianne L.. "Aviles Street". Paranormal Activity Network Information Center Database. PANICd.com. www.panicd.com/aviles-street.html. 1 Jan. 2011. Web. 9 Aug. 2017.

"Aviles Street". First Coast News. Tegna Co. www.firstcoastnews.com/news/local/news-article.aspx?catid=3&storyid=155560. n.d. Web. 1 Feb. 2011.

Saint Augustine Jail

Donley, Shawn A.. "Saint Augustine Jail". Paranormal Activity Network Information Center Database. PANICd.com. www.panicd.com/old-st-augustine-jail.html. 1 Aug. 2017. Web. 13 Aug. 2017.

"Old Jail". Visit St. Augustine. Visitstaugustine.com. www.visitstaugustine.com/thing-to-do/old-jail. n.d. Web. 1 Aug. 2017.

"Saint Augustine Haunted Places, Saint Augustine Jail". HauntedHouses.com. Haunted Houses, Inc. www.hauntedhouses.com/states/fl/saint-augustine-jail.htm. n.d. Web. 13 Aug. 2017.

"Haunted Guide to the Old Jail". Ghost and Gravestones. Historic Tours of America, Inc. www.ghostsandgravestones.com/st-augustine/old-jail.php. n.d. Web. 13 Aug. 2017.

Bayfront Marin House (Bed and Breakfast)

"St. Augustine History at a Glance :: Stylish Bayfront Marin House." Bayfront Marin House. N.p., n.d. Web. 03 Aug. 2017. http://www.bayfrontmarinhouse.com/st-augustine-history.html

"St. Augustine – A Ghostly Encounter." Ghosts | haunted places | cemeteries | ghost stories. N.p., n.d. Web. 03 Aug. 2017. http://www.ghosthaunts.com/st_augustine.html

Huguenot Cemetery

Donley, Shawn A.. "Huguenot Cemetery". Paranormal Activity Network Information Center Database. PANICd.com. www.panicd.com/huguenot-cemetery.html. 13 Aug. 2017. Web. 13 Aug. 2017.

"Huguenot Cemetery". Wikipedia. Wikimedia Foundation, Inc. en.wikipedia.org/wiki/Huguenot_Cemetery. 3 Apr. 2017. Web. 13 Aug. 2017.

"Haunted Guide to the Huguenot Cemetery in St. Augustine". Ghost and Gravestones. Historic Tours of America, Inc. www.ghostsandgravestones.com/st-augustine/huguenot-cemetery.php. n.d. Web. 13 Aug. 2017.

O.C. White's Pub

Donley, Shawn A.. "O.C. White's Pub". Paranormal Activity Network Information Center Database. PANICd.com. www.panicd.com/oc-whites-pub.html. 12

Aug. 2017. Web. 12 Aug. 2017.

"Location and History". O.C. White's Restaurant. O. C. White's Seafood and Spirits . www.ocwhitesrestaurant.com/location-and-history/. n.d. Web. 12 Aug. 2017.

"Saint Augustine Haunted Houses, O.C. White's Pub, HauntedHouses.com". HauntedHouses.com. Haunted Houses Inc.. www.hauntedhouses.com/states/fl/oc-whites.htm. n.d. Web. 12 Aug. 2017.

"Hauntings". O.C. White's Restaurant. O. C. White's Seafood and Spirits . www.ocwhitesrestaurant.com/hauntings/. n.d. Web. 12 Aug. 2017.

Harry's Seafood, Bar & Grille

Donley, Shawn A.. "Harry's Seafood, Bar & Grille". Paranormal Activity Network Information Center Database. PANICd.com. www.panicd.com/harrys-seafood-bar-and-grille.html. 13 Aug. 2017. Web. 13 Aug. 2017.

"Catalina's Ghost". Weird U.S.. Weird NJ inc. weirdus.com/states/florida/ghosts/catalinas_ghost/index.php. n.d. Web. 13 Aug. 2017.

"A Haunting Experience at Harry's". Ghost Augustine. GhoSt Augustine Tours & BEERHAMMERS Store. ghostaugustine.com/2010/05/21/a-haunting-experience-at-harrys/. n.d. Web. 13 Aug. 2017.

Old Drugstore

Donley, Shawn A.. "Old Drugstore". Paranormal Activity Network Information Center Database. PANICd.com.

www.panicd.com/old-drug-store.html. 13 Aug. 2017. Web. 13 Aug. 2017.

"Old Drug Store". NationsOldestCity.com. The Nation's Oldest City. www.nationsoldestcity.com/old-drug-store/. 1 Mar. 2010. Web. 13 Aug. 2017.

"Haunted Tour of St. Augustine by Ghosts & Gravestones". Ghost and Gravestones. Historic Tours of America, Inc. www.ghostsandgravestones.com/st-augustine/gravestones-ghost-tour.php. n.d. Web. 13 Aug. 2017.

Casa Monica Resort and Spa

Donley, Shawn A.. "Casa Monica Resort and Spa". Paranormal Activity Network Information Center Database. PANICd.com. www.panicd.com/casa-monica.html. 13 Aug. 2017. Web. 13 Aug. 2017.

"Casa Monica Resort and Spa". Historic Hotels of America. National Trust of Historic Preservation. m.historichotels.org/basicphone/index.php/property/history?id=casa-monica-resort-spa. n.d. Web. 13 Aug. 2017.

"Casa Monica Hotel Haunted". Fright Find. Fright Find. frightfind.com/casa-monica-hotel/. n.d. Web. 13 Aug. 2017.

McGlothlin, J. "Casa Monica Hotel". Mystery411.com. McGlothlin Industries Inc. www.mystery411.com/Landing_casamonicahotel.html. 1 Nov. 2013. Web. 13 Aug. 2017.

Flagler College

"Ponce de Leon Hotel". Wikipedia. Wikimedia Foundation, Inc.

en.wikipedia.org/wiki/Ponce_de_Leon_Hotel. 18 Aug. 2009. Web. 13 Aug. 2017.

Donley, Shawn A.. "Flagler College". Paranormal Activity Network Information Center Database. PANICd.com. www.panicd.com/flagler-college.html. 13 Aug. 2017. Web. 13 Aug. 2017.

"Flagler College Hauntings, Saint Augustine". HauntedHouses.com. Haunted Houses, Inc. www.hauntedhouses.com/states/fl/flagler-college.htm. n.d. Web. 13 Aug. 2017.

Morales , Christina Marie. "Flagler College". Ghost Stories of Saint Augustine, Florida. Blogger. saintaugustineghosts.blogspot.com/p/flagler-college.html. n.d. Web. 13 Aug. 2017.

Infantes, Nicole. "Ghost Stories Of Flagler College". Odyssey. Odyssey Media Group, Inc.. www.theodysseyonline.com/ghost-stories-of-flagler-college. 25 Jul. 2016. Web. 13 Aug. 2017.

"Room 300". Your Ghost Stories. YourGhostStories.com. www.yourghoststories.com/real-ghost-story.php?story=6985. 18 Aug. 2009. Web. 13 Aug. 2017.

"Haunted Florida - Flagler College St. Augustine". Greatest Unsolved Mysteries. greatest-unsolved-mysteries.com. www.greatest-unsolved-mysteries.com/haunted-florida.html. n.d. Web. 13 Aug. 2017.

Casablanca Inn

Donley, Shawn A.. "Casablanca Inn". Paranormal Activity Network Information Center Database. PANICd.com. www.panicd.com/casablanca-inn.html. 18 Aug. 2017.

Web. 18 Aug. 2017.

"Casablanca Haunted Hotel - St. Augustine".
HauntedHouses.com. Haunted Houses Inc.
www.hauntedhouses.com/states/fl/casablanca-inn.htm.
n.d. Web. 18 Aug. 2017.

"The Casablanca Inn in Haunted St. Augustine".
HauntedPlacesToGo.com. HauntedPlacesToGo.com.
www.haunted-places-to-go.com/casablanca-inn.html. n.d.
Web. 18 Aug. 2017.

Oldest Wooden School House

Donley, Shawn A.. "Oldest Wooden School House".
Paranormal Activity Network Information Center
Database. PANICd.com. www.panicd.com/oldest-
wooden-school-house.html. 18 Aug. 2017. Web. 18 Aug.
2017.

"Oldest Wooden Schoolhouse in the United States".
OldestWoodenSchoolHouse.com.
oldestwoodenschoolhouse.com.
www.oldestwoodenschoolhouse.com/. n.d. Web. 18 Aug.
2017.

"Visitor Information". OldestWoodenSchoolHouse.com.
oldestwoodenschoolhouse.com.
www.oldestwoodenschoolhouse.com/VisitorInformation/
index.htm. n.d. Web. 18 Aug. 2017.

Bjorkman, Sue. "Where History Lives: Oldest Wooden
Schoolhouse educates visitors on Menorcan heritage".
staugustine.com. The St. Augustine Record.
staugustine.com/news/local-news/2014-11-17/oldest-
wooden-schoolhouse-educates-visitors-menorcan-heritage.
17 Nov. 2014. Web. 18 Aug. 2017.

INDEX

Abela, Captain Manuel 49

Alcazar Annex..........106

Andreu, Joseph 16

Apopinax tree............34

Aviles Street 57

Bayfront Boarding House 127

Casa Monica Hotel ..106

Casablanca Inn 128

Castillo de San Marcos 47

Cathedral-Basilica of St. Augustine 32

Chief Tolomato........100

coquina 14

Cordova...................106

Cubo Line 42

Dark of the Moon........4

de Porras, Catalina 91

dry moat....................48

Elizabeth....................43

Flagler, Henry 59, 63

Fort Marion 48

Genoply, Juan..........134

Gomaas, Antonio 97

Hotel Alcazar 106

Juanillo, Don............100

Junior Service League of St. Augustine, Inc. .15

Kessler, Richard C....107

Mantanzas Hotel.....127

Marti, Colonel Garcia 49

Marti, Dolores 49

Minorcan...................31

Morgan, James P.......35

ABOUT THE AUTHORS

Shawn and Marianne Donley live in Youngstown, Ohio. The have been together and traveled on adventures since 2003, but their paranormal experiences, interest, and research did not fully begin until 2010 with the creation of the PANICd.com database.   Since this time, they have traveled to various places across the United States that have paranormal claims and conducted research on these locations.   They have participated in many historical and ghost tours and have collected a wealth of information that will be organized and presented in this series of books called, "Our Haunted Travels."

Shawn and Marianne Donley

www.ingramcontent.com/pod-product-compliance
Lightning Source LLC
Chambersburg PA
CBHW030012110426
42741CB00032B/330